EARLY YEARS ACTIVITY CHEST

Fund raising activities

British Library Cataloguing-in-Publication Data
A catalogue record for this book is available from the British Library.

ISBN 0 439 98314 2

The rights of Kevin Kelman and Susan Smith to be identified as the authors of this work has been asserted by them in accordance with the Copyright, Designs and Patents Act 1988.

DEDICATION
For Kristian and Daisy

ACKNOWLEDGEMENTS
The publishers gratefully acknowledge permission to reproduce the following copyright material:

Sally Scott for 'The graduation song' © 2002, Sally Scott, previously unpublished; **Susan Smith** for 'The picture hunt' © 2002, Susan Smith, previously unpublished; **Brenda Williams** for 'The broken promise', 'Things to do at the fun-fair!', 'A hand to touch' and 'These feet' © 2002, Brenda Williams, all previously unpublished.

Every effort has been made to trace copyright holders and the publishers apologize for any inadvertent omissions.

AUTHORS
Kevin Kelman and Susan Smith

EDITOR
Jane Bishop

ASSISTANT EDITOR
Lesley Sudlow

SERIES DESIGNER
Lynne Joesbury

DESIGNER
Martin Ford

ILLUSTRATIONS
Shelagh McNicholas

COVER PHOTOGRAPH
Martyn Chillmaid

Text © 2002 Kevin Kelman and Susan Smith
© 2002 Scholastic Ltd
Designed using Adobe Pagemaker
Published by Scholastic Ltd, Villiers House,
Clarendon Avenue, Leamington Spa, Warwickshire CV32 5PR
Printed by Alden Group Ltd, Oxford
Visit our website at www.scholastic.co.uk

1 2 3 4 5 6 7 8 9 0   2 3 4 5 6 7 8 9 0 1

CONTENTS

CONTENTS

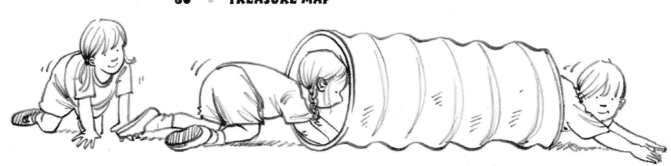

Introduction

This book forms part of a series which provides ideas for a range of activities across all of the six Areas of Learning encompassed in the Early Learning Goals for pre-school children.

Practical suggestions for organizing fund-raising events in early years settings are provided. The fund-raising events listed in this book involve the children in a range of stimulating activities, provide excellent opportunities to strengthen home links and enhance relationships between staff and parents as well as generating funds to supplement other income within early years groups.

As far as possible, each event has opportunities for the children to be actively involved while others are more adult-focused. However, each of the events is supplemented with exciting ideas that will ensure the children can become involved, as part of their daily routine within their setting.

Involving the children

Make sure that the children feel involved right from the start of each fund-raising event. Tell them about the events that you have planned and explain how their group will benefit. In many instances, the children themselves can be given a role or responsibility in the fund-raising event, for example, children can be involved in the selection of dressing-up costumes to be purchased with the proceeds of the fashion show (page 40) or in selecting books that they would like to buy with the proceeds of the book fair (page 21).

In order to keep children motivated to learn, we must offer them a variety of experiences that engage their interest. Likewise, when organizing fund-raising events, we must vary them to generate interest within the community. This book suggests events that can be opened to the wider community and will bring a range of people together. In this way, the children's sense of community and citizenship can be broadened, for example, inviting residents from the local sheltered housing complex to attend a Ladybird drive brings young and old people together and can be beneficial to all involved in the event.

Above all else, the events are aimed to help keep the fun in fund-raising. When you organize events make sure that the focus is not just on making money but also about making sure that people enjoy themselves, too. People are more likely to contribute if they are in an environment where they feel relaxed and are enjoying themselves. The best outcome for fund-raising events is that they are seen as positive and entertaining occasions which people actually look forward to, as well as giving everyone involved with the group, a common goal.

How to use this book

There are seven chapters, each covering important aspects of fund-raising within early years groups. These provide users involved in fund-raising with practical suggestions of how to make fund-raising successful and, most of all, fun. The chapters are arranged to give a quick reference of ideas into which you might dip for inspiration, confident that the fund-raising ideas are tried and tested and that the supporting activities are linked to the requirements of the Early Learning Goals. The supporting activities suggested can be applied equally well to the documents on pre-school education published in Scotland, Wales and Northern Ireland.

Chapter 1 offers tips on fund-raising, including how to get donations, planning and organizing events, as well as an ideas bank of additional fund-raising activities.

Chapters 2 to 6 explain how to organize a wide range of fund-raising events. Chapter 2 focuses on sponsored events that are very straightforward to organize. Each individual event directly involves the children, giving them the chance to practise specific skills and, therefore, promoting learning.

Chapter 3 outlines a range of fairs and fêtes that involve families and the wider community. These provide opportunities to celebrate seasonal events such as Christmas or midsummer.

In Chapter 4, details are given on raising funds through the sale of a wide range of merchandise. Opportunities to buy goods such as photos, tea towels and calendars that make ideal gifts for family and friends can be provided by following the suggestions listed.

Social events are covered in Chapter 5. These involve families and provide events for the social calendar of the local community. Events such as these help to raise the profile of the group within the local area.

Chapter 6 looks at everyday fund-raisers – ideas that can be used quickly and easily in any situation. These can be dipped into, in response to a particular need, to raise funds.

For each event listed within Chapters 2 to 6, suggestions are given on What you need, Preparation and What to do, as well as a Checklist of key tasks to be completed by organizers. Three supporting children's activities are listed for each event. These supporting activities ensure that the children within the group are meaningfully involved in relevant learning experiences linked to the fund-raising events. The supporting activities require the minimum of preparation and resources and are designed to allow users to dip in and select as appropriate.

Chapter 7 gives a list of helpful addresses and contacts for those involved in fund-raising, including charitable trusts and other sources of funding. Details of additional publications that may benefit fund-raisers in early years settings are also listed. Additionally, this chapter looks at the importance of the role of charity sponsorship where the children help local charities, perhaps a children's hospital or nationwide appeals seen on television, such as Red Nose Day or Children in Need.

Photocopiable pages

A selection of the photocopiable sheets such as 'Shape scene' (page 69) and 'Ladybird drive' (page 76) are required for the children to use as part of the fund-raising events. In addition, there are sheets provided to support the organization of the events such as the 'Christmas hamper' list (page 72) and the 'Children's Christmas hamper' list (page 73). Others such as 'Animal snap' (page 71) and 'Cups and saucers' (page 77) are designed as resources to be used for one specific supporting activity.

Finally, there are also photocopiable sheets containing a song, stories and rhymes that are designed to appeal to young children.

Using resources

It is a good idea to have a fund-raising storage box containing basic items such as books of cloakroom tickets, empty money bags, plastic float tubs and bunting, all of which can be used at many of the events.

The activities in this book require resources that are readily available to most early years groups. Often, the event can be adapted to suit the resources that are available to your group such as in the 'Obstacle course' activity (page 14). However, some events require specific resources that can be obtained from specialist fund-raising companies that are listed in Chapter 7. Resources such as face paints or large playing cards (page 28) can be safely stored away for use at future events.

Throughout the book, specific story-books are referred to in the supporting activities and these will all be readily available from major bookshops. Some supporting activities, for example, 'Hook a duck' (page 27) or Sounds tubs (page 15) require resources to be made by adults before beginning the activity. In addition there are occasions when you can ask the children to bring in resources needed for an activity, for example, 'Find the pair' (page 19) requires the children to bring in pairs of socks or gloves from home.

Links with home

For any fund-raising event to be successful within an early years setting, strong parental support and involvement is necessary. Encourage parents to participate in fund-raising events from the outset and announce forthcoming activities on the notice-board or in newsletters. Many of the events highlighted in this book require adult volunteers to help them run smoothly. This can be a very positive way to pull together parents, staff, children and the community at large.

Parents should always be made aware of how much their efforts are appreciated by the group. This can be done in a variety of ways including thank-you notes, newsletters outlining the success of a specific activity, posting names of helpers or donors on the notice-board or giving out fun certificates which acknowledge a family's involvement and support.

Ensure that you take a sensitive approach to the children whose parents may not wish to be as involved as others. Also be aware of the amount of 'giving' you ask of parents during the year. Carefully consider the planning of the events in order not to inundate parents with requests for donations in a short period of time. You are more likely to gain support if parents know they are raising money for something that has a special significance for the group and from which their child will directly benefit from.

Planning ahead

At the start of a new session, make provisional plans for the fund-raising events for the year. By doing this you can ensure that events are spread evenly across the year and fit in with seasonal or festival considerations, for example, organize a photographer's visit (page 30) so that orders are returned to the group in time for Mother's Day and can make suitable gifts for mothers and grandmothers, or circulate Webb Ivory catalogues (page 58) so that items arrive in time to be given as Christmas presents. By planning the session's fund-raising events in advance you can also ensure that you will have funds available for specific goals, for example, Christmas presents, summer outings and so on.

Follow these useful tips to achieve a successful fund-raising event. Organization and planning are the keys to success and you will find that you will soon reap the benefits. Involve as many people as possible and make your fund-raising events pleasurable occasions.

Fund-raising tips

All pre-school settings will benefit from having a fund-raising team. This group should be made up of both staff and parents where possible. Larger groups may have a fund-raising committee with specific responsibilities such as chairperson, treasurer, secretary and publicity officer.

Organizers and helpers

Whatever your group's situation, you will require organizers and helpers for each fund-raising event. Organizers need to have plenty of time to spare, whereas helpers may be too busy with other commitments to organize but willing to help on an *ad hoc* basis. Organizers should keep an up-to-date list of available helpers and their contact details.

Many people are more willing to help on a rota basis at any event so that they can also participate in events with their own families. Do not forget to invite other family members to become helpers – grandparents and older children often have more time to spare than working parents.

Planning, organizing and evaluating

Careful planning is essential for effective fund-raising. The co-ordinator of each event should be well organized, ensuring that all the necessary preparations are in place. Organizers should take specific responsibilities for events and the activities in this book include useful checklists to help them successfully implement each fund-raising event.

Consider drawing up a schedule planner to determine when jobs need to be completed and by whom. This will aid the smooth running and success of the fund-raising event.

After each event, keep records of how successful it was so that you can monitor the effectiveness of the activities and determine if an event is worth repeating in future years. If something has not been successful, organizers should try to determine why – is there something that could have been done differently to ensure success? Will the event have to be replaced by an alternative activity next year?

Throughout the year, keep a record of the total raised with proceeds individually itemized. Remember to offset any costs, so that a true indication of your net profit is shown. An excellent way to collate this information is to create a fund-raising file that can be added to and updated. It may be helpful to also store contact names and addresses of previous business sponsors, fund-raising catalogues, details of photographers used in the past, sample posters/tickets for events, pro forma sponsor forms and hamper lists in the file. This file can also be passed on for use by new fund-raisers over the years.

Legal implications

It is essential to consider legal requirements when planning fund-raising events. The responsibility for ensuring that events planned are carried out legally lies with the organizers. It is advisable to find someone locally who can give you up-to-date and accurate legal advice as laws frequently change. Local authorities often have legal departments willing to advise early years groups.

Some of the main areas to seek legal advice on when planning fund-raising events include:

• Food hygiene – contact your local Environmental Health Department.
• Second-hand goods – contact your local consumer advice office, bearing in mind it is not advisable to sell electrical goods.
• Gaming or Liquor Licence – contact The Charity Commission (see page 58) for further information.
• Music Licence – contact the Performing Rights Society.

Additional information on legal requirements and obtaining licences can be obtained from your local library, the Citizen's Advice Bureau, the National Council for Voluntary Organizations (in Scotland – the Scottish Council for Voluntary Organizations) or the Gaming Board for Great Britain.

Insurance

Renew the group's policy annually and be aware of the insurance cover provided.

Publicity

Appoint an orgzanizer to take overall responsibility for all publicity and ensure that any calls or queries can be directed to them. Parents may have access to suitable publishing programs on their personal computers so it is worth asking them for assistance.

Posters, fliers or adverts produced should include the name of the group, type of event, date, time, place, entrance fee, special attractions and the purpose of fund-raising. Ask the local community to display these in shops, schools, libraries, clinics, dentists' and doctors' surgeries. Make posters more durable to display outdoors by laminating pieces of card. An ideal way to publicize an event is to send out fliers to individual households. Often, local scouts groups or newsagents will deliver these for a nominal fee.

Contact local newspapers, which are likely to have an events column and a wide local readership, with details of forthcoming events, inviting a photographer to come along on the day if appropriate.

Prizes

Many of the activities described in this book refer to awarding prizes. You will need to give careful consideration to what these prizes should be and how you will obtain them. If an activity is likely to have several winners, or is relatively cheap to take part in, then a prize worth a few pounds or less is suitable. If the participation cost is higher, or the chances of winning less, a more valuable prize may need to be provided.

Options for obtaining prizes include:

• Asking parents for donations – this is usually successful but do not rely on this for every event as parents may grow tired of being asked to donate items regularly.

• Buy small prizes such as sweets or items from specialist companies such as Baker Ross or Peeks (see pages 57 and 58). When you purchase prizes for events ensure that your expenditure can be easily offset against the projected income so that a healthy profit is still made.

• Write to local businesses inviting them to sponsor or donate a prize. Make it clear that they will be mentioned in any publicity material. Adapt this sample letter (below) to suit your particular circumstances. Always acknowledge replies and donations with a letter of thanks and a copy of any publicity materials. It is also worth while keeping a note of the details of previous sponsors in your fund-raising file for future reference.

Name of group
Address
Contact telephone number
Date

Dear Sir/Madam (or contact name, if known)
Name of Group
Prize Draw

Our pre-school group is situated in the outlying area of Anytown and is made up of over fifty children aged between three and five years old.

Fund-raising is required to help provide our group with various 'extras' and to help meet ongoing costs. This term we aim to provide a set of 25 tabards embroidered with the group's name and logo. This will enhance the security of the children on group outings as they will be more easily identifiable.

To this end, we are holding a Spring Fling Dance on Friday, 21 March 2003, and the prize draw will be an important fund-raising focus during the course of the evening.

We would be immensely grateful if you could contribute a prize for our draw or donate something towards our goal.
(Company name) would of course be listed as a supporter of the group when the draw is made and mentioned in any publicity relating to this event.

I hope you will consider our plea kindly.
Please do contact me with any queries you may have.
Yours sincerely

Jones

Mrs J Jones
Group Secretary

Prices

You will need to decide on an entrance fee or ticket price for each fund-raising event. Bear in mind what will be included in this fee. There are several options open to groups that include:

• Setting a low fee, which is purely for entry.
• Charging slightly more, but giving a cloakroom ticket which enters the buyer into a prize draw.
• Charging a higher fee but including refreshments such as tea, coffee and biscuits within this price.

Family and friends are generally happy to pay a higher cost to watch the children participate in a show or concert. When organizing a more costly event such as a dance or supper, look closely at your outgoings before setting a ticket price to ensure that a profit is made.

Sponsor forms

Make and issue sponsor forms well in advance of any relevant events. This allows families the opportunity to make contact with their family and friends before the event takes place to seek sponsors. Always make it clear what the event is for and allow sponsors the opportunity to give a specific amount as a donation, rather than sponsoring the child per lap or per item.

A to Z of fund-raising events

Within chapters 2 to 6 there are 44 fund-raising events described. Together with the ideas listed below this gives you 100 to choose from.

A
Aerobathon
Auction

B
Bingo night
Bounceathon

C
Caption competition
Car wash
Cheese and wine
Cookery demonstration

D
Donkey derby
Duck race

E
Easter egg hunt
Exhibition of art

F
Football match
Fun run

G
Games evening
Golf tournament

H
Hair shave
Holiday change
(spare currency)
Hurl the haggis

I
International night
It's a knockout

J
Joke book
Jumble sale

K
Karaoke night
Kidnap (and 'ransom')

L
Leap for charity
Lucky dip
Lucky straws (roll up cloakroom tickets)

M
Mile of pennies
Mystery tour

N
Name that tune night
Non-uniform day

O
One-day fast
One price stalls

P
Parachute jump
Pocket money stall
Pot luck evening

Q
Quazar night
Quiz night

R
Raft race
Roll-a-dice

S
Silent auction
Spot the baby (photos)
Supermarket trolley dash

T
Teddy bears picnic
Trampoline marathon

U
Undo a lock

V
Valentine's party
Variety show

W
Whist drive
Whodunnit murder evening

X
Xmas carol singing
Xmas cards

Y
Yellow day (dress in yellow)
Yesterday's news (guess the year)

Z
Zipline for charity

Have fun with these sponsored activities and raise money for your setting at the same time! The children will enjoy asking their family and friends to sponsor them for the different events such as the 'Readathon, 'Fill a matchbox' and 'Growing sunflowers'.

Sponsored events

CHECKLIST

Inform parents of the event and how they can help their children to collect coloured items.

• • • • • •

Issue sponsor forms.

• • • • • •

Ensure that sponsor forms are completed and returned before the event.

• • • • • •

Sign sponsor forms to verify the children's participation.

• • • • • •

Issue certificates to recognize the children's achievements.

• • • • • •

Set a deadline for returning sponsor money.

ELMER'S COLOURS

What you need
Elmer by David McKee (Red Fox); colour cards showing different shades of paint (from your local DIY store); template of elephant; A4 paper; scissors; glue; laminator or plastic wallets; sponsor forms.

Preparation
Read one or two of the Elmer stories to the children. Discuss the stories and focus on the different colours on Elmer's coat. Give each child a colour card and invite them to find something in your room that matches the colour exactly. Make a table-top display with the Elmer books you have read, the colour cards and the matching items. Draw an elephant shape on a sheet of A4 paper and copy one for each child.

What to do
Provide each child with an elephant shape, cut the colour cards into 3cm squares and invite the children to glue ten different-coloured squares on to their elephant to make an Elmer pattern. Laminate their elephants or place them in plastic folders for protection. The children are sponsored to gather items at home that match the colours on their Elmer sheet.

Different types of elephant books
Communication, language and literacy
Talk about why Elmer wanted to be like other elephants and what was different about him. Look at information books about elephants. Encourage the children find the name of a baby elephant.

Hide and seek
Knowledge and understanding of the world
Stick the children's completed Elmer pictures around your room. Let the children go and 'hunt' for their own. Discuss why it was easy to find them. Look at nature magazines to find examples of natural camouflage and discuss why animals need camouflage in their natural environments.

Paint mixing
Creative development
Fill paint pots with primary colour poster paints. Encourage the children to create their own colours by mixing the primary colours. Invite them to add small amounts of black or white poster paint and to observe the changes that take place. Use the shades to make Elmer paintings.

OBSTACLE COURSE

What you need

Beanbags; hoops; low benches; plastic tunnel; blanket; floor trampolines or similar apparatus; sponsor forms.

Preparation

Consider the space available and the resources that the group can access. Decide which stations you will use to form a circuit. Some suggested stations are:

• Crawl through a tunnel or under a blanket.
• Throw a beanbag into a bowl.
• Lift a hoop over your head.
• Hop along the line.
• Walk along a low bench.

What to do

Let the children practice using obstacle courses during physical development sessions. The children are sponsored to complete the obstacle course. On the day of the sponsored event, allow each child to work their way around the course while the other children cheer and encourage their peers.

The hare and the tortoise
Communication, language and literacy

Read *The Hare and the Tortoise* by Aesop (Traditional) to the children. Discuss how the story does not finish as you might expect. Explain to the children what is meant by the term 'the moral of the story' and encourage them to relate it to everyday situations.

Beanbags and hoops
Mathematical development

Gather a range of coloured beanbags and ask the children to sort them into sets of different colours. Use beanbags for practical counting activities. Place coloured hoops in an open space and invite the children to place the beanbags that match the colour of the hoops inside them.

Planning the course
Knowledge and understanding of the world

Discuss with the children the kind of activities that could be used in the obstacle course. Invite them to give their own suggestions. Draw a rough plan of the obstacle course on frieze paper using pictures of different pieces of equipment cut from old magazines. Label each activity on the plan. Encourage the children to use a programmable toy to go from station to station.

A BAGFUL OF SOUNDS

What you need
Carrier bags (paper or plastic); marker pen; range of everyday items; cloth bag; sponsor forms.

Preparation
Play 'I spy' encouraging the children to take turns at the game identifying items around your room. Gather a range of everyday items in an attractive cloth bag and pull the items out one at a time and ask the children which sound each item begins with.

What to do
Give each child a carrier bag with a letter drawn on the outside of it. Use the most common sounds avoiding q, u, v, x, y and z. The children are then sponsored to gather as many items as they can from home that begin with their allocated sound, placing the items in their carrier bags and bringing them in so that the items can be checked and counted.

My bag
Personal, social and emotional development
Give each child a copy of the photocopiable sheet on page 68 and ask them to each write the letter that starts their name on their bags. Encourage the children to personalize their bags with pictures and drawings of things that are important to them. Invite the children to talk to the others in the group about the things that they have drawn and why they chose them.

Sounds bingo
Communication, language and literacy
Make bingo cards with five rows and four columns. Write a selection of letters of the alphabet (in lower case) in ten of the boxes, blanking out the other ten boxes. Explain the rules of the game to the children and play bingo together. Let the children take turns at being the bingo caller.

Sounds tubs
Communication, language and literacy
Collect empty 250g tubs from supermarkets and write a different letter of the alphabet (in lower case letters) on each tub. Gather a range of small plastic toys and items that will fit into the tubs, for example, in the 'b' tub you may have a badge, a balloon, a doll's bag and a toy bus. Take two of the tubs and mix up the contents, then invite the children to sort them again.

READATHON

What you need

A wide range of children's story-books, comics, children's poetry books; sponsor forms.

Preparation

Compile a newsletter telling parents about the 'Readathon' that you are planning and ask for their support in reading stories, comics and so on to their children at home during the readathon week. Produce a sponsor form ensuring there is a large enough space for the children to draw a small picture about each story they have enjoyed. The children can be sponsored for each book that they listen to over the period of a week.

What to do

During the readathon week, allow the children to choose several books from your collection, or from home for adults to read to them. As an alternative, provide story tapes for the children to listen to as they look at the book. Invite the children to draw a picture on their sponsor form to record each text that they have listened to.

Book awareness
Communication, language and literacy

Each time you read a book to the children, model the use of language such as the title, author, cover, illustrator and so on. Read several books by the same author and ask the children if they notice any similarities in the texts. Emphasize to the children that it is important to handle books carefully when they are reading them.

How many books?
Mathematical development

Make a simple picture graph to show how many books by particular authors the group have read. After reading a book to the children, ask one child to copy the cover of the book on to paper then add it to the graph on the wall.

Seasonal bookmarks
Creative development

Take the children on an outdoor walk to gather seasonal materials that could be used to make bookmarks, for example, collect sycamore seeds, fallen leaves and small twigs. Provide the children with strips of coloured card and invite them to glue on their collected seasonal items. When they are dry, let the children use them as bookmarks.

CHECKLIST
Inform parents of the event and how they can help their children to collect items.

• • • • • •

Issue sponsor forms.

• • • • • •

Ensure that sponsor forms are completed and returned before the event.

• • • • • •

Sign sponsor forms to verify the children's participation and how many items they have found.

• • • • • •

Issue prizes or certificates to recognize the children's achievements.

• • • • • •

Set a deadline for returning sponsor money.

FILL A MATCHBOX

What you need
An empty matchbox for each child in the group; an empty apple box; an empty shoebox; poster paint; paintbrushes; glue; glitter; small sticky shapes and sequins; sponsor forms.

Preparation
Show the children an empty apple box, an empty shoebox and an empty matchbox and talk about the difference in size of the boxes. Invite the children to take turns at finding something in the room that would fit into each of the boxes. Talk about the space left in each box. Ask the children to consider the best way to get many items in each box and encourage them to identify that they should put lots of smaller items in rather than one or two bigger items.

What to do
Give each child an empty matchbox. Invite them to paint their matchboxes, then decorate them by sticking on glitter, sequins and shapes. Explain to the children that when they take their boxes home, they should try to fit as many items as they can into their matchboxes. Give the children some ideas to start them off such as a pine needle, a blade of grass, a stamp and so on. Collect all the boxes in after a week. Let the children explore the contents of the different boxes with you and add up how many different things they have found.

My special box
Personal, social and emotional development
Decorate a matchbox and pass it around during circle time, inviting each child to say what they would keep in this special little box and why. Adapt the activity to encourage the children to talk about wishes, for example, 'I wish I could go inside this special box and find…'.

Sort them out
Mathematical development
Gather a range of different-sized cardboard boxes with lids and let the children enjoy trying to match the lids and boxes or fitting the boxes inside one another.

Squeeze in!
Physical development
In a large, open space, ask the children to imagine that they are trying to squeeze into as small a space as possible. Vary it to include large spaces, long, narrow spaces and so on.

FIND THE SHAPES

What you need
Material bag with plastic shapes in it (include circles, squares, rectangles and triangles); crayons or colouring pencils; a copy of the photocopiable sheet on page 69 for each child; sponsor forms.

Preparation
Gather the children in a circle and invite them, one at a time, to take a shape from the bag. Encourage the children to name the shape and challenge them to see if they can find something in the room that is the same shape.

What to do
Give each child a copy of the photocopiable sheet which includes a range of basic shapes on the picture. Encourage the children to work together to spot two or three shapes, then allow them to work individually to find more. The children are sponsored to find and colour as many of the shapes as they can on the picture. This event should be carried out within the group as an everyday activity.

Bear in a square
Communication, language and literacy
Read *Bear in a Square* by Stella Blackstone (Barefoot Books) to the children. The story introduces shapes and encourages the children to find and identify a range of brightly-coloured shapes. Let the children take turns at turning the pages and asking the others in the group which shapes they can spot.

Food shapes
Mathematical development
Make toast and invite the children to cut it into triangle- or rectangle-shaped snacks. Use cake cutters to make circle-shaped sandwiches. Look at other food things that are shaped such as cheese triangles, burgers, sliced meats, samosas or apple turnovers. (Check for any food allergies and dietary requirements.)

Snap happy!
Knowledge and understanding of the world
Go outside to look at buildings in the local area. Ask the children to look for familiar shapes. Point to circular windows or rectangular wall plaques. Let the children take photographs of shapes in their local environment. Display the photographs within the group setting. The activity may be developed to make pictures of buildings using sticky shapes.

RAINBOW DAY

What you need

A simplified version of the story of 'Noah's Ark' such as in *The Usborne Children's Bible* retold by Heather Amery (Usborne); different colours of diluting juice; different colours of fruit (green apples, red apples, black grapes, oranges, blueberries and so on); sponsor forms.

Preparation

Let parents know that you are planning a sponsored 'Rainbow day' during which the children will be encouraged to wear as many different-coloured clothes as they can, for example, a red sock and a green sock, a yellow polo shirt, blue trousers, an orange hat and so. Explain to parents that they should certainly not buy new items of clothing just for this event! The children are sponsored per colour of the rainbow that they wear.

What to do

Include as many activities relating to rainbows or colour on the day as possible, for example, start the day by singing 'I can sing a rainbow', re-tell the story of 'Noah's Ark', have different-coloured fruit snacks and drinks at snack time and so on. Break the day's activities into specific colours, for example, say the action rhyme 'Ten Green Bottles', then let the children experiment with green gloop and so on.

My name is Will and I am wearing a blue jumper, red shorts and yellow socks!

My name is...
Personal, social and emotional development

Gather the children to form a circle and invite each child to celebrate their attempt at wearing a variety of colours. Invite them to say to the group 'My name is Amy and I am wearing a red jumper, green socks' and so on.

Rainbow words
Communication, language and literacy

Encourage the children to have fun making up alliterative phrases about colours such as green grapes, purple plants, yellow yo-yos, blue buses and so on.

Find the pair
Mathematical development

Ask parents to donate socks and gloves that the children have outgrown. Place them in a washing basket and invite the children to match the pairs of socks and gloves. Make it more challenging by including different sizes of the same colour or type of socks.

GROWING SUNFLOWERS

What you need

Sunflower seeds; compost; large, plastic, soft-drink bottles (cut in half); plant markers (old ice-lolly sticks are ideal); other examples of seeds; sponsor forms.

Preparation

Show the children the different kinds of seeds, for example, apple seeds, sycamore seeds, melon seeds and sunflower seeds. Let the children touch, feel and smell the seeds. Warn the children not to eat them or put them in their mouths or up their noses.

What to do

Explain to the children that they are going to plant their own seeds and look after them. Give each child two sunflower seeds to plant. Set a date for the children's plants to be measured and issue sponsor forms so that the children can gather sponsors for each centimetre that their tallest plant grows.

Word fun
Communication, language and literacy

Talk about the word 'sunflower'. Gather a selection of pictures and photographs of sunflowers. Tell the children why the plant was given its name. Discuss other words that are made up of two smaller words. Chop words in half and try to find their partner, for example, ever + green = evergreen; sun + shine = sunshine; car + wash = carwash; up + stairs = upstairs and so on.

How tall are you?
Mathematical development

Make fingerprints, handprints and footprints to create sunflower picutres. Use brown finger-paints to create seeds and yellow handprints for petals. Use green footprints for the stalk and leaves. Let the children try to make their sunflower the same height as themselves. Display these on the wall using various lengths of garden cane as the stalks. Use the display to develop the children's mathematical language, for example, tallest, shortest, taller than, as tall as, and so on.

Science fun
Knowledge and understanding of the world

Experiment to see if seeds will grow in any condition or if they need light, water and soil. Set up the experiment, for example, pot one – soil, no light, no water; pot two – water, light, no soil; pot three – soil, water, no light; pot four – soil, water and light. Discuss and record the results of the experiment.

Fairs and fêtes can be a good source of fund-raising, providing a fun event and bringing the local community together. Ideas in this chapter include a Spring Fair, Christmas Fair and a general selection of stalls that can be used anytime at different fund-raising events.

Fairs and fêtes

CHECKLIST
Inform parents of the event and gather as many volunteers as possible.

• • • • • •

Appeal for donations of books, tapes, videos, records and CDs.

• • • • • •

Use posters to advertise locally.

• • • • • •

Print tickets and sell them in advance.

• • • • • •

Check the condition of all items donated before selling.

• • • • • •

Categorize and group items.

• • • • • •

Organize floats.

• • • • • •

Organize refreshments.

• • • • • •

Thank parents and inform them of the amount raised.

BOOK AND RECORD FAIR

What you need
Tables; card; pens; tubs of change; plastic carrier bags; posters; tickets; refreshments; volunteers.

Preparation
Gather donations of books, records, videos, tapes or CDs and check that they are in good condition. Sort them into categories such as 'Romance', 'Mystery', 'Children's' and so on. Make labels from card stating the genre. Organize refreshments to sell during the event. Decide on an entry fee.

What to do
With the children's help, set up each stall with books, records and CDs carefully displayed. Ensure that each stall or area has a float, noting the amount. Place empty carrier bags at each stall for those buying several items. Set up an area with tables and chairs where refreshments can be served. Ensure that someone is on the door selling tickets.

Make your own book
Communication, language and literacy
Using the template and instructions on the photocopiable sheet on page 70, encourage the children to draw pictures showing a simple sequence of events, for example, my day, the life of a butterfly or playing a game. Ask the children to write a simple sentence for each picture, if appropriate.

The local library
Knowledge and understanding of the world
Arrange a visit to the local library and show the children how it is set up. Discuss how the books are grouped into a children's section, fiction and so on. If possible, arrange for the children to each borrow a book and to make a follow-up visit a week or two later to return or change the books.

The sound of music
Physical development
Discuss the different sorts of music that the children know and then let them listen to examples such as reggae, pop, classical and jazz. Ask them to think of the kind of movement that each sound evokes and use words to describe it, for example, fast and busy, slow and graceful, strong and slow. Invite the children to express themselves through movement in which ever way they feel best fits each piece of music.

SPRING FAIR

What you need
Various stalls; posters; tickets; cloakroom tickets; refreshments; a compère; volunteers.

Preparation
Discuss the different seasons with the children, highlighting the features of each one. Inform them that you will be holding a Spring Fair. Sell tickets in advance, if possible.

What to do
Organize a variety of stalls and activities for the children and adults. Sell tickets at the door. Invite local craft people to participate for a percentage of sales, or a flat rate. Ideas for stalls and activities are listed on page 28.

Further seasonal activities may include:
- Plant stall – Ask for labelled, potted cuttings from parents.
- Pancake stall.
- Crème eggs stall – Bury hard-boiled eggs in the sand tray. Invite participants to take a bowlful of sand and if they find an egg, they win a crème egg.
- Find the matching halves – Make card egg shapes. Invite the children to decorate them and then cut them in half as if they were cracked. Jumble them up in an appropriately-decorated box. Invite participants to put their hand into the box and select two halves. If they match, they win a prize.
- Easter bonnet parade – Invite the children to make home-made bonnets. Advertise the event by posters in advance and award every participant a certificate.
- Sell raffle tickets. Suggestions for prizes are given on page 10.

Animal families snap
Knowledge and understanding of the world
Discuss spring and new life, plants growing and animals giving birth to their young. Introduce the correct vocabulary for the young of farm animals. Using the photocopiable sheet on page 71, preferably laminated, explain to the children that in this game of snap they must pair an adult animal with its young.

Coloured daffodils
Knowledge and understanding of the world
Bring in some daffodils for the children to see. Talk about their colour and name the different parts of the flower – stem, leaves, petals and so on. Place some flowers into a vase of water and add red or blue food colouring to the water. Let the children observe and record any changes over the next few days.

Old MacDonald
Creative development
Use this idea to introduce new vocabulary for the names of baby animals. Sing 'Old MacDonald had a farm' but use the baby animal names, for example, 'Old MacDonald had a farm, and on that farm he had a foal.'

CHECKLIST

Inform parents of the event and gather as many volunteers as possible.

• • • • • •

Use posters and the local press to advertise.

• • • • • •

Print tickets and sell them in advance.

• • • • • •

Invite outside stallholders.

• • • • • •

Organize floats.

• • • • • •

Buy refreshments.

• • • • • •

Obtain presents/ prizes.

• • • • • •

Organize a Santa Claus outfit.

• • • • • •

Thank all involved and inform them of the amount raised.

CHRISTMAS FAIR

What you need

Various stalls and activities; Santa Claus outfit; posters; tickets; refreshments; cloakroom tickets; volunteers.

Preparation

Invite local craftspeople to participate. Display a copy of the hamper lists on the photocopiable sheets on pages 72 and 73 and invite parents to sign alongside something that they will provide. Make up hampers ready to raffle them. Organize refreshments and allocate a 'catering' team.

Ask someone, who is willing, to be Santa and organize to hire a costume. Order presents for the grotto through companies such as Baker Ross or Peeks (see pages 57 and 58).

What to do

Plan a range of stalls, ensuring that there are plenty of activities for the children themselves. Stalls and activities could include:

- Candles.
- Christmas cards.
- Santa's grotto.
- Decorations.
- Pin the tail/antlers on Rudolph.
- Any local craft – Christmas wreaths, stockings or salt-dough decorations.
- Raffle for Christmas hampers.

Sell tickets on the door to include refreshments such as mulled wine, mince pies or Christmas cake. Set up the grotto and have presents marked either boy or girl with an age range, for example, 'Boy 1–2 years'.

Presents for the birds
Personal, social and emotional development

Stress the fact that Christmas is a time for giving and thinking of other people. Encourage the children to think about how difficult it is for animals and birds in the wild to find food in the cold, dark, winter months. Make bird presents by mixing warmed lard (heated by an adult) with birdseed, nuts, chopped apple and diced bread. Pack this mixture into small, empty yoghurt pots that have a long twig poked through them. Use twine to hang outside once set.

List to Santa
Communication, language and literacy

Discuss who Santa Claus is, where he lives and what he does. Ask each child to name something that they hope he will bring them. Invite an adult to scribe a Christmas list with the children contributing ideas. Cut and stick pictures from seasonal catalogues to illustrate the list.

Handprint angel cards
Creative development

Show the children how to paint one hand white and make two prints, palms overlapping to form wings. Show them how to make a third handprint to form an angel's body. Let the children dip a finger into flesh-coloured paint and add a round head above the body. Once dry, they can draw in a face using a black pen and add a halo with a glitter pen. Stick the angels onto folded card and sell them at the fair if desired.

TABLE-TOP/CAR BOOT SALE

What you need
Posters; tables; an outdoor area for car boot sale; a co-ordinator.

Preparation
Advertise in advance to attract sellers and buyers on the day. Decide how many pitches you can offer and whether these will be indoor, outdoor or both. Give each space a number and prepare a plan.

What to do
When sellers contact you, note down their details, allocate them a number and mark them on your plan. Inform them that no electrical goods should be sold (see page 10). Decide how much the fee will be for each pitch and consider asking for payment on booking, in case people do not turn up on the day.

On the day, the co-ordinator should have the plan with all the details. Make sure that someone is available to greet each arrival, check them off on the plan and direct them to their space.

Looking after our community
Personal, social and emotional development
Discuss the sale with the children, explaining that many of the items sold will be toys, books or games that someone no longer wants. Explain how, if items are still in good condition, someone else can have fun with or make use of them. Introduce the term 'recycling', using clothes handed down between family and friends as an example. Ask the children to identify other items which their family recycles such as paper, glass and so on. Discuss what they think the benefits of this might be.

The sale role-play
Mathematical development
Explain how the table-top sale works and what might be sold. Set up the role-play area as a table-top sale and set out books, games and clothes labelled with prices. Invite the children to take on the role of seller or browser and let them use plastic or card coins in place of real money.

Make fridge magnets
Creative development
As the focus is on recycling, encourage the children to save their crisp packets. Invite them to bring a selection in and then bake them in the oven at around 150°C for 20 minutes. This causes them to shrink and harden. Once the crisp packets have cooled, glue small magnets to the back to make fridge magnets. These can be sold at the fair with profits going to the group.

HEALTH AND FITNESS FAIR

What you need

Large hall; representatives from local clubs/sports facilities; tickets; healthy snacks and refreshments.

Preparation

Organize a venue large enough to host the planned event. Contact local sports clubs and organizations, leisure centres and hobby groups explaining the event you are planning. Invite them to attend to represent their group and tell them the proposed date. Explain that they can use the event to advertise their club in order to attract new support and members.

Organize related stalls and activities such as 'Beat the goalie' or have a raffle for an autographed football. Advertise the event throughout the community and send information leaflets home with the children for their families and friends.

Buy healthy snacks to sell at the fair. Ensure that you have enough volunteers.

What to do

Sell tickets for the event through local outlets if possible and through parents at your group. On the day, prepare the hall or venue ensuring that all the groups have the space they will need.

Clubs represented could include netball, badminton, tennis, swimming, athletics, dancing, martial arts, hillwalking, photography, cooking – depending on what is available locally. Check whether there is a line dancing, tap or gymnastics club who will put on a display at the event.

Sell the healthy snacks and refreshments.

Sort the balls
Mathematical development

Provide a variety of different balls. These could include marbles, table-tennis balls, golf balls, tennis balls and footballs. Ask the children to order them according to size. Introduce size vocabulary and encourage observations such as 'it is smaller than the football, but bigger than the golf ball'.

Healthy foods
Knowledge and understanding of the world

Ask the children to think about the food that they eat. Which of these foods do they think might be good or bad for them? Provide them with pictures of food, cut from magazines, and ask them to sort them into healthy and unhealthy and to stick the pictures onto a 'healthy' paper plate and an 'unhealthy' one. Display the plates and discuss as a group.

Healthy exercise
Physical development

When telling the children about the health fair, explain how important it is to be active and to exercise. In a large, open space give the children the opportunity to develop ball-handling skills such as rolling, kicking and throwing. Allow them to use different sizes and types of ball.

CHECKLIST
Inform parents of the event.

• • • • • •

Approach a variety of party plan companies and confirm the planned date.

• • • • • •

Use poters to advertise locally.

• • • • • •

Send out invitations.

• • • • • •

Obtain raffle prizes.

• • • • • •

Thank all those involved for their support and inform them of the amount raised.

PARTY PLAN EVENING

What you need
A variety of party plan representations (see page 58); posters; invitations; cloakroom tickets; raffle prizes.

Preparation
Contact a variety of party plan firms such as Tupperware, PartyLite or The Body Shop. Decide on a date, time and suitable venue. Confirm the donation to the group with each representative (possibly 10% commission on sales) depending on the product.

Advertise the event, emphasizing that there will be no pressure to book a party. Organize a raffle and display the prizes.

What to do
Send invitations to parents. Sell raffle tickets in advance and on the night. Confirm each representative's attendance and ensure that they arrive in time to set up. Emphasize that there must be no pressure on browsers to book a future party. Set up the raffle and draw winners at the end of the evening.

Who would you invite?
Personal, social and emotional development
Discuss parties, where they are held and who attends. Ask each child what kind of party they would like to have. Suggest an ice-cream party, a Tweenies party, Barbie party and so on. Then discuss who they would invite to the party and why.

Thank-you letters
Communication, language and literacy
Ask the children if they send thank-you letters for the gifts that they receive on their birthdays or at Christmas. Have they ever received a thank-you letter? Discuss the importance of thanking someone who has thought about you. Ask the children to write thank-you letters to the people who demonstrated at the event. Print a small standard 'thank-you' note and attach it to the children's emergent writing notes.

Make party invitations
Creative development
Draw balloon shapes ônto brighty-coloured pape. Ask the children to cut them out and decorate on one side with glitter, sparkly stars and collage materials. On the reverse, write an invitation to your event containing all the relevant details. Attach a piece of ribbon to the bottom of the balloon and send them to the local primary school, the church, other pre-schools or nurseries and so on. Ask them to display them on their notice-board.

FAMILY FUN FAIR

What you need

Suitable indoor/outdoor venue; posters; barbecues; face paints; a compère; music; thick rope for the Tug-of-war; range of stalls/activities; volunteers; loudspeaker.

Preparation

Advertise the event in advance with posters, a flyer or by placing an advertisement in the local newspaper. If you are holding a fancy-dress competition, give advance notice. Organize volunteers, inviting parents to sign a rota so that help is provided in shifts. Ask people who would be willing to dress as clowns to give out balloons and so on. Invite a local personality to open your event. Ask a parent to provide and organize a barbecue on the day, cooking food to sell.

Invite local community groups to enter teams into the Tug-of-war and charge £5 per team. Suggest that they dress in something representative of their group. Obtain prizes (see page 10).

What to do

The compère should begin the proceedings. Display a rough programme of events so that people know, for example, that the fancy-dress competition is at 2.30pm and so on.

Ideas for stalls and activities are Tombola, Lucky dip, Hook a duck, Balloon race, Hoopla stall, Wet sponge throw, Wheel of fortune, Roll a penny and Races for adults and children.

What's fun?
Personal, social and emotional development

Discuss the different things that the children do with their families to have fun. What do they find enjoyable and why? As a follow up to your discussion, read *Tidy Up, Trevor* by Rob Lewis (Bodley Head Children's Books).

Action rhyme
Communication, language and literacy

Read the action rhyme 'Things to do at the fun-fair!' on the photocopiable sheet on page 66 to the children. Invite them to join in the words and actions. Ask them for other suggestions to add to the action rhyme.

Hook a duck
Physical development

Ask the children to help you cut out duck shapes from card and then fasten a metal paper clip onto each beak. Make simple fishing rods using sticks, string and a small magnet tied to the end. Invite the children to hook a duck. Develop the game further, by putting coloured dots or shapes onto the underside of the ducks. Declare the winner the person who has the most ducks with red dots and so on.

CHECKLIST

Inform parents of the event.

• • • • • •

Use posters to advertise locally.

• • • • • •

Print tickets and sell them in advance.

• • • • • •

Organize prizes .

• • • • • •

Thank all those involved for their support and inform them of the amount raised.

INDOOR AND OUTDOOR STALLS

This selection of stalls can be used at a variety of fund-raising events.

Face painting/body art – Invest in good-quality face paints which are easier to apply, remove and kinder to the skin. Although, initially, they will cost more, you should recover costs quickly. If possible, have two or three face painters at a time. Nail decorating is also popular – buy glitter and transfers to use.

Play your cards right –Buy a pack of large playing cards, lay out seven in a row, face down. Invite participants to correctly predict whether the next card is higher or lower than the previous one – 'and you don't get anything for a pair'!

Bottle stall – Collect bottled donations (fizzy drinks, juice, water, wine, beer, shampoo and so on). Separate and fold one half of a book of cloakroom tickets and put them into a bucket or box. Attach tickets ending in 0 to 5 from the other half of the book to each bottle and discard the rest of the tickets. Invite participants to pay per draw. If a ticket drawn matches one on a bottle they win that prize (adults only to collect alcohol).

Find the key – Obtain a padlock and ask a locksmith to make 30 keys similar to the correct one. Place the keys into a cloth bag and shake. Charge £1 to pick a key and try the lock. The correct key wins a prize.

Ball in jar – Place empty glass jars in rows on a table. Invite participants to stand behind a line and pay to throw three table-tennis balls into the jars. If a ball goes into a jar, they win a prize.

Roll a penny – Draw concentric circles, similar to a target, on to card. Value each ring. Decrease the distance between circles as you near the centre – with five circles the values could be 1, 3, 5, 7 and 10 for the bull's-eye. Charge for rolling three 1p pieces. A score of 18 or more wins a prize. Coins lying across lines do not count. Display the rules clearly.

Catchy names

Communication, language and literacy

Ask each child to think of the sound at the start of their names. Can they find a describing word beginning with the same sound? Give an example, such as 'Friendly Fiona' or 'Happy Harry'. If they are successful, encourage them to create names for the stalls and display signs on the day, for example, 'Tom's Terrific Tombola', 'Kristian's Crafty Keys' and so on.

Making bunting

Mathematical development

Show the children how to make bunting by cutting large shapes from activity paper. Attach the sections to a long piece of string and ask the childen to think about the pattern being made, considering colour as well as shape.

Role-play

Creative development

Let the children pretend to be stallholders. Prepare simple stalls such as 'Roll a penny' or 'Ball in a jar' (use plastic tumblers). Discuss what they might say to attract customers, for example, 'Roll up, roll up!', 'Fabulous prizes to be won' and so on. Can the children entice others to participate?

Carry out these activities during your usual meeting time, where the children can be directly involved in producing various items of merchandise to raise money for your group.

CHECKLIST
Send off for information packs from several manufacturers.

● ● ● ● ● ●

Inform parents of the event and gather orders.

● ● ● ● ● ●

Complete appropriate paperwork and send off order.

● ● ● ● ● ●

Make a display to advertise the tea towels within your group.

● ● ● ● ● ●

Set deadline for returning money.

● ● ● ● ● ●

Thank parents and inform them of the amount raised.

Merchandise

GROUP TEA TOWELS

What you need
A variety of patterned tea towels; fine black felt-tipped pens; mirrors; photographs of the children.

Preparation
Contact some of the companies that produce tea towels listed in Chapter 7 on page 57 and 58.

What to do
Show the children the range of tea towels that you have gathered. Talk about what they are used for and look at the different designs on them. Explain to the children that they are all going to work together to produce a group tea towel and that everyone in the group will have a drawing of themselves on the tea towel. Invite the children to bring in recent photos of themselves to look at and encourage them to describe their features. Next, invite the children to look closely at themselves in the mirror. Give each child a small piece of paper and ask them to draw a self-portrait, encouraging them to use the mirror to look at the different parts of their heads as they are drawing.

Follow the instructions that the manufacturers send to you on how to organize the necessary artwork in order to send it to them. Gather orders for the tea towels, bearing in mind that most manufacturers reduce the cost with larger orders. Sell the tea towels at a price that will ensure you make a profit.

Washing up
Personal, social and emotional development
When the children have finished their snack or baking activity, encourage them to help wash the dishes. Support the children to use a tea towel to dry the dishes, explaining to them the importance of holding the dish with one hand while drying with the other.

Sort the washing
Mathematical development
Place several tea towels and some items of clothing in a washing basket. Invite the children to sort the washing, separating the tea towels from the other clothes. Extend this activity by asking individual children to take two tea towels from the basket, or two blue tea towels and one red, and so on.

Looking at materials
Knowledge and understanding of the world
Gather a range of pieces of material, such as denim, plastic, cotton and silk, each measuring approximately 10cm by 10cm. Test the materials to see which absorbs water best and, therefore, would make good tea towels.

Contact local group photographer.

• • • • • •

Inform parents of photographer's impending visit.

• • • • • •

Set a date for final orders to be submitted.

• • • • • •

Complete appropriate paperwork and send off order.

• • • • • •

Set deadline for returning money and ensure that unwanted photographs are returned.

• • • • • •

Thank parents and inform them of the amount raised.

PHOTOGRAPHS

What you need
Photographer; chairs or benches for children to stand on for group photographs.

Preparation
Contact one of the many companies that specialize in children's portrait and group photographs. These should be listed locally in the Yellow Pages.

What to do
Inform parents that you have organized a photographer to come to the group. Ask them if they would like individual, family or group photographs. Ensure that the parents know when they have to bring in their other children if they want a family photograph. Clear a space that the photographer may use without being disturbed. Take extra care when children are getting on and off benches and chairs for group photos.

Distribute the photos as soon as they are returned from the photographer with clear guidance about prices, ordering more photos and returning unwanted photos.

Say cheese!
Mathematical development
Allow the children to take photographs of one another. Mount the photographs and make a birthday train with each carriage representing a different month of the year. Put the photographs on the appropriate train carriage.

Looking at materials
Knowledge and understanding of the world
Gather a range of photographs, both black and white and coloured. Encourage the children to look closely at what is shown in the photographs to see if they can sort them into sets of old and new. Make this activity more challenging by photocopying the colour photographs and then asking the children to sort them into old and new.

You have been framed!
Creative development
Make framed photographs by gluing a photograph to a piece of thick card, large enough to leave a border around the photograph. Cut four pieces of card that fit on to the size of the border. Invite the children to glue a range of types of pasta onto their strips of card. When the glue has dried, paint on a mixture of gold powder paint and PVA glue to get a shiny finish. Finally, glue the strips onto the border around the photograph. These can be displayed within the group to create 'Our picture gallery'.

CHECKLIST

Make ready-prepared cards that the children can print straight on to.

• • • • • •

Inform parents of the event and gather orders.

• • • • • •

Set deadline for returning money.

• • • • • •

Thank parents and inform them of the amount raised.

A HANDPRINT OR A FOOTPRINT

What you need

A copy of the photocopiable sheet on page 65; A4 paper or card; washable poster paints; aprons; shallow food trays; laminator.

Preparation

Choose to make either handprints or footprints. Copy the photocopiable sheet, cut out the chosen poem and stick it in the centre of a piece of A4 paper. Make an attractive border approximately 1cm from the edge of the piece of paper. Photocopy the page onto card to provide a copy for each child in the group.

What to do

Working with a small group, ask the children to put on aprons. If you plan to do the footprint poem remove the children's footwear and socks. Gather the children and give each child one of the pieces of card prepared earlier. Invite them to dip their hands or feet into the trays of poster paint and then help them to make prints at either side of the poem on the card.

Leave the prints to dry, write the child's name and the date on the card in the spaces provided and laminate. These prints can then be sold to parents, grandparents and other family friends as souvenirs and keepsakes.

Helping hands
Personal, social and emotional development

Make an award by drawing around a child's hand on card, laminating it and attaching a piece of wool to create a medal. Talk about 'helping hands' and give the award to children that help others without having to be asked.

Talking hands
Communication, language and literacy

Place a range of teddy or doll-sized clothes in a rucksack without the children seeing them. Place your hand in the rucksack and describe an item of clothing without bringing it out. When a child guesses the item correctly, invite them to put their hand in the bag to describe an item of clothing that they can feel to the rest of the group. Let each child have a turn at describing.

Hands and feet
Creative development

Make up a song with the children about the things that we can do with our hands and feet:

We can all clap, clap, clap, clap, clap, clap
with our hands.
We can all wave, wave, wave, wave, wave, wave
with our hands.
We can all run, run, run, run, run, run
with our feet.
We can all stamp, stamp, stamp, stamp, stamp, stamp
with our feet... and so on.

OUR COOKBOOK

What you need
Word processor; paper; fine, black felt-tipped pens; computer graphics package; posters.

Preparation
Ask parents, carers, children, staff and local community members to each give you a copy of their favourite recipes. Local celebrities may also like to be involved in an initiative such as this.

What to do
Once all the recipes have been gathered, sort them into sections, for example, Soups and starters, Main courses, Desserts, Baking and Children's cookery. Use a word-processing package and type up the recipes in an A4 format. Use some of the children's black line drawings and illustrations from a computer graphics package, such as Clip Art, to illustrate the recipe book. Reduce the page size on a photocopier to A5 format to cut down on reproduction costs.

In the introduction to the book thank everyone involved and explain what the proceeds of the sale of the book will go towards. Local businesses may give you a contribution towards the cost of producing the book in return for a small advertisement in it.

Organize a book launch and invite local press to publicize the book. Sell the book through parents, staff, local shops and other businesses.

Rhyming recipes
Communication, language and literacy
Look at recipe books with the children and explain the standard layout of a recipe with the ingredients, method and so on. Have fun making up revolting recipes and give each creation a title. As an extension to the activity, make up alliterative names for dishes such as 'Paul's Purple Pumpkin Pie'.

Weighing
Mathematical development
Make some of the recipes that you have collated. Give the children responsibility for weighing and measuring the ingredients, using a variety of methods to include spoonfuls, weighing with scales and using a measuring jug.

My favourite dinner
Creative development
Invite the children to look through old magazines and supermarket fliers to find foods that they like to eat. Give each child a paper plate. Invite them to cut out their own pictures and encourage them to stick them onto the plate. Display these on the wall and make them into place settings using plastic cutlery.

CHECKLIST
Send off for
information packs
from several
manufacturers.

• • • • • • •

Inform parents of
the event and
gather orders.

• • • • • • •

Use posters to
advertise the
calendars within
your group and the
local community.

• • • • • • •

Set a date for final
orders to be
submitted.

• • • • • • •

Complete
appropriate
paperwork and
send off order.

• • • • • • •

Set deadline for
returning money.

• • • • • • •

Thank parents and
inform them of the
amount raised.

CALENDARS

What you need

A collection of commercially-produced calendars; fine, black felt-tipped pens; posters.

Preparation

Contact one of the many companies that use children's drawings to produce calendars listed in Chapter 7 on pages 57 and 58.

What to do

Invite the children to look through the calendars that you have gathered. Explain to them what the function of a calendar is and ask them if they know which month their birthday is in. Tell the children that the group is going to make their own calendar.

As a group, decide on the style of calendar that you wish to produce. It will be more personal and more attractive to parents if you include their children's own drawings. You may choose to make the calendar as an A3 sheet containing a small drawing from each child at the top, and the months and so on printed on the bottom half. As an alternative, you may wish the calendar to be 12 separate pages with larger drawings from individual children. Follow the instructions that the manufacturers send to you on how to organize the necessary artwork in order to send it to them. Gather orders for the calendar and sell them at a price that will ensure you make a profit.

A cheaper option is to make your own calendar and then enlist the help of your local school or business to laminate them for you.

Chinese calendar
Personal, social and emotional development

Explain to the children that in the Chinese calendar each year is named after an animal. Talk about the festivities of Chinese New Year and find out which animal represents the years that the children were born: 1996 – Rat ; 1997 – Ox; 1998 – Tiger; 1999 – Rabbit; 2000 – Dragon.

Yesterday, today and tomorrow
Communication, language and literacy

To help develop the children's concept of time, make a 'Yesterday, Today and Tomorrow' frieze. Create signs with Velcro backing, with the names of the days of the week that can be attached to the frieze and changed on a daily basis. Add pictures and words to show activities that the group do on a particular day.

My week
Knowledge and understanding of the world

Encourage the children to use a word processor to type the days of the week. Print them off and ask the children to draw a picture beside each day to show something that they usually do on that day.

FAVOURITE SONGS AND POEMS

What you need
Blank tapes; tape recorder; microphone; the photocopiable sheet on page 74.

What to do
Select which of the songs and poems in the group the children enjoy best and would like to have on their group cassette and involve the children in the decision-making process. (If a CD is preferred, see details for the company 'Sound sense' on page 58.) Make simple pictograms to show which songs and poems are the favourites within the group.

Record the children singing their favourite songs and reading their favourite poems on to a tape using a microphone and tape recorder over a few days. Keep a record of the order in which they are recorded. Make multiple copies of the recording using a twin-deck tape recorder.

Type or write the order on to the cassette cover on the photocopiable sheet. Photocopy the cover and invite the children to each personalize their covers by filling in their names and making a drawing on the front.

The final compilations can then be sold to parents and carers so that the children can share them at home or in the car.

Karaoke kids
Communication, language and literacy
Invite the children to choose a song or poem that they like and encourage them to sing or say it to the rest of the group. Support any children who are singing or speaking by joining in with them.

Recording sounds
Knowledge and understanding of the world
Provide the children with opportunities to use a tape recorder to record themselves singing or talking. Play it back to them and see if they can recognize one another's voices. Develop this activity by allowing the children to tape different sounds inside and outside the group setting.

Making instruments
Creative development
Create some simple musical instruments to accompany the children's recordings, for example, make a guitar from an empty tissue box and elastic bands, or a tambourine using a paper plate and small bells tied onto it. Make shakers from tubs with different grains or pulses inside them.

TEDDIES WITH T-SHIRTS

What you need
A selection of T-shirts with designs on; A4 white paper; scissors; colouring pencils; fabric pens or paints and paint-it-yourself teddies from the company 'All My Own Work' (page 57); posters.

Preparation
Send off for information packs. Order enough paint-it-yourself teddies for each child in the group to have one. Cut out T-shirt shapes approximately 15cm wide from white paper.

What to do
Gather several T-shirts with a range of attractive designs including self-coloured T-shirts with no designs. Discuss the designs with the children, asking them which ones they like best and why. Give each child a T-shirt-shaped piece of paper and invite them to design their own T-shirt on it. On a one-to-one basis, help the childrent to transfer their design using fabric pens or paints onto the T-shirts supplied by the commercial company. When they are dry, allow the children to put the T-shirt that they designed on to one of the teddies. Sell these to parents to raise funds for your group.

Additional orders can be made with individual's names printed on the teddies as gifts. This would be an ideal stocking filler and orders could be taken from within the local community.

Sad teddy, happy teddy
Personal, social and emotional development
Use the photocopiable sheet on page 75 to play the 'Teddy bear emotions game'. Copy, colour and laminate the teddy and various faces on the sheet and then tell the children a story about a teddy that involves feelings, for example, 'Ted woke up in the morning and heard a noise downstairs, how do you think he felt?'. Let the children choose the appropriate face for the teddy at different stages in the story.

Colourful T-shirts
Mathematical development
Cut out large T-shirt shapes from and invite the children to use potato prints to create interesting patterns on the T-shirts. Display these on a rope suspended across the room, attaching them with clothes pegs.

Moving teddies
Knowledge and understanding of the world
Cut out paper teddy shapes and arms and legs that can be attached using split pins. Allow the children to draw on T-shirts, similar to the ones that they have designed.

OUR YEARBOOK

What you need
Large pieces of black fabric; camera; access to a photocopier.

Preparation
Plan the compilation of a yearbook well in advance so that you can gather pieces of appropriate material throughout the time that the children attend your group. Cut out cape-shaped pieces from the black fabric.

What to do
Gather a variety of pieces of work by the children, record transcripts of children's discussions and take photos of the children working to make a yearbook. Ensure that each child has work represented within the yearbook. Involve the children in the design of the publication. Ask local companies for sponsorship in return for a small advert in the yearbook. Make photocopies of the completed book and add a ribbon to the spine to make it look special.

At the end of the academic year, if appropriate, organize a 'graduation ceremony' at which the children are presented with certificates and a keepsake gift to mark the end of their time in your group. Invite parents along and provide refreshments. Make simple cloaks by attaching a cape-shaped piece of black material to the children's clothes.

Sell the yearbook and tickets to the 'graduation ceremony' to parents and other family members. Organize an 'official' photographer – this may be a member of staff or parent – to take individual and family portraits. Invite the local press along to take photographs and to write a report on the event.

Memories
Personal, social and emotional development
Talk about how the children feel to be leaving the group and moving on to another group or school. Encourage the children to talk about the memories that they have from their time with you. Share some of your memories from working with them too.

We're moving on!
Creative development
Practise singing 'The graduation song' on the photocopiable sheet on page 67 for the 'graduation ceremony'. Invite the children to use simple percussion instruments as an accompaniment to the chorus.

Graduation hats
Creative development
Make hats by cutting a square of thick cardboard approximately 25cm by 25cm. On the underside glue on a strip of cardboard approximately 5cm wide that fits the circumference of the child's head. Let the children paint the hats black and attach a black tassel.

Organize your social events so that they are fun and entertaining occasions. People will look forward to them and enjoy themselves as well as raising money for a good cause.

CHECKLIST
Inform parents of the event.

• • • • • • •

Use posters to advertise locally.

• • • • • •

Print tickets and sell them in advance.

• • • • • •

Make copies of the photocopiable sheet on page 76.

• • • • • •

Arrange pencils, dices and so on.

• • • • • •

Organize refreshments.

• • • • •

Organize prizes.

• • • • •

Thank parents and inform them of the amount raised.

Social events

LADYBIRD DRIVE

What you need
The photocopiable sheet on page 76; posters; tickets; several dice; pencils; tables and chairs; refreshments.

Preparation
Inform parents of the proposed date and time of the event. Advertise locally with posters. Sell tickets in advance, so that you know how many people to expect and how many copies of the game sheet, dice and pencils you will need. Refreshments can either be sold on the night or included in the ticket price. Sell tickets at the door as well, and be prepared for extra participants. Set tables and chairs to cater for groups of between four and six people.

What to do
Each player in the teams will need a copy of the photocopiable game sheet and a pencil, and each team will need a dice. Players take turns to roll the dice and mark on the section of the ladybird they score each time. The first person to complete their ladybird is the winner. You can either have a winner at each table in each round or an overall winner – the first to complete a ladybird out of all the people present. Prizes can be given for each game or for the overall winner on the night.

Story-book
Personal, social and emotional development
Read *The Bad-Tempered Ladybird* by Eric Carle (Hamish Hamilton) and look at the illustrations. Discuss how the ladybird was behaving. How did the other creatures feel? Ask the children how they like to be treated and highlight the importance of considering other people's feelings.

Counting spots
Mathematical development
Help the children to draw or paint ladybirds onto pieces of A4 card (one per card) but do not add spots at this stage. Once the shapes are completed, ask the children to stick circles of black paper onto their pictures, ensuring that each has a different number of spots, between one and ten. When they are dry, mix the cards up and ask the children to try sequencing them according to the number of spots.

Minibeast hunt
Knowledge and understanding of the world
Take the children to a park or wooded area. Discuss how tiny creatures are all around, but that often we do not notice them. Working in pairs or small groups, let the children hunt for minibeasts. Stress the importance of treating them with care and returning them to their natural habitat. Let the children use magnified viewers to observe the minibeasts.

AUCTION OF PROMISES

What you need
A suitable venue; posters; chairs; auctioneer or compère; gavel or similar; lists of 'lots'; volunteers; refreshments.

Preparation
Contact parents and other people connected with the group and write to local businesses or associations, informing them of the details of the auction. Invite them to donate items or promises that will be auctioned off at an event. Promises could include two hours of ironing, providing a 'taxi' service for a night out, four hours of babysitting or cooking a family meal for four. Individuals may have talents that could be put to use such as writing a customized poem or making a sketch of a pet. Circulate a list so that volunteers can write down their 'promise'. Add any promises received from local businesses and print a final list of numbered lots.

Ask someone to be a compère who will run the auction and select approximately six volunteers to help at the event. Advertise the event in the local area and through the local press.

What to do
On the day, set out rows of chairs for the audience with one for the auctioneer or compère at the front facing them. Photocopy the lists of lots and give them to people as they arrive. The auctioneer or compère should begin the proceedings, detailing the lot and suggesting a starting offer. Bids are taken, with volunteers placed to help spot bidders, and each promise is sold to the highest bidder. Volunteers will need to note the details of each successful bid next to the relevant lot number on the list.

Put the donors of each promise in contact with the successful bidder so that they can make any necessary arrangements. Have a break during the event in which you can sell refreshments.

Keeping a promise
Personal, social and emotional development
Talk about promises that the children could make and keep at home for a week. Make a note of what each child decides. Promises might include helping to tidy toys, cleaning teeth twice and day and so on. Send home a note to parents explaining what their child has promised. At the end of the week, ask parents to sign and return the note, commenting on how well the promise was kept.

A broken promise
Communication, language and literacy
Read the story 'The broken promise' on the photocopiable sheet on page 63 to the children. Discuss the consequences and how the characters felt. Encourage the children to talk about promises that they have made or that other people have made to them.

An auction
Knowledge and understanding of the world
Explain to the children what an auction is and how it works. Role-play an auction, with some of the toys that you have, thinking about the roles of auctioneer, helpers and bidders.

CHECKLIST

CHECKLIST
Inform parents of the event.

• • • • • •

Prepare treasure hunt, noting time and distance, and keeping a copy of the answers.

• • • • • •

Photocopy treasure hunt and maps of area, if needed.

• • • • • •

Use posters to advertise locally.

• • • • • •

Organize a prize for the winning team.

• • • • • •

Make a list of items to collect in the event of a tie.

• • • • • •

Thank all those involved for their support and inform them of the amount raised.

FAMILY TREASURE HUNT

What you need
Copies of map of area covered; copies of treasure hunt; prize; posters.

Preparation
One or two adults will need to create the treasure hunt, deciding whether it will be completed on foot or in a car and set the hunt accordingly. The clues could be cryptic and you could ask questions about something you find at each location. Print the clues on a sheet, leaving space for the team name and the answers to be written. Work out how long you expect the whole hunt to take and organize a prize for the winning team.

What to do
Advertise the treasure hunt within your group and the local area. Specify that it is for adults and children in teams of two to five people, and open to all. Inform people of the date, time and meeting point and whether it is to be completed by car or on foot and, if on foot, whether it is suitable for buggies. Charge each group for a copy of the treasure hunt. Let teams know where the finish or gathering point is and what the time limit is.

Allocate points for each correct answer and the team with the most points wins. Ask entrants to collect certain items that could be taken into account if there is a tie on points. Items could include a feather, a yellow flower and so on.

Treasure hunt story
Communication, language and literacy
Read the book *Sonny's Treasure Hunt* by Lisa Stubbs (Piccadilly Press) to give the children an understanding of what a treasure hunt is. Then, organize a simple hunt, similar to Sonny's, that the children can complete in pairs, with adult supervision. These are more fun held outdoors if possible.

Using a programmable toy
Knowledge and understanding of the world
Tape large sheets of wallpaper together and, on the reverse, let the children draw treasure in different places. Using a programmable toy, allow the children to give instructions to try to reach the treasure from the starting point.

Making treasure
Creative development
Show the children how to create treasure by making coin rubbings using gold, silver and bronze crayons. They can also paint uncooked pasta tubes with metallic paint and thread them onto string to make necklaces or chains.

CHECKLIST

Inform parents of the event and gather as many volunteers as possible.

• • • • • •

Use posters and local press to advertise.

• • • • • •

Print tickets and sell them in advance.

• • • • • •

Organize models, helpers and a compère.

• • • • • •

Organize refreshments.

• • • • • •

Thank all those involved for their support and inform them of the amount raised.

• • • • • •

Return the clothes.

FASHION SHOW

What you need
A suitable venue; chairs; volunteers; adult and child models; clothes; compère; catwalk area; posters; tickets; camera; refreshments; music system and CDs or tapes.

Preparation
Invite local clothes shops or supermarkets to lend clothes for a fashion show. Ask parents to volunteer themselves and their children as models. Work out a running order, organize a simple script for the compère and prepare background music. Hold a practice and time the fashion show, allowing models time to change. Ask for helpers behind the scenes to care for the clothes and to help change the models. Advertise the event in the local area. Design, print and sell tickets.

What to do
Set out chairs for the audience leaving a catwalk area. Borrow temporary staging if possible, though this is not necessary. Sell tickets both in advance and on the night. Provide members of the audience with a leaflet itemizing the clothes and prices. Invite a representative of the retailer to be present to take orders.

Invite the compère to present the show, using a helper to play the music as planned. Have an interval in which you can sell refreshments. Take photographs during the event that can be sold or given out later.

Describing textures
Communication, language and literacy
Gather a range of clothes of different textures such as silk, lamb's wool, cotton, suede and leather and place them in a suitcase. Encourage the children to each pull out a piece of clothing and to describe how it feels, for example, smooth, soft, scratchy, furry, tickly and so on. Help them to develop their language skills by encouraging the rest of the group to suggest alternatives or to add their own ideas.

What will fit?
Mathematical development
Make a display of different-sized clothes and toys. These could include clothes for teddy bears, baby dolls and Barbie-style dolls. Discuss them with the children and encourage them to decide which clothes would fit which toy best. Develop the children's mathematical language by using words such as 'long', 'short', 'bigger than', 'smaller than' and so on.

Practice makes perfect
Physical development
Gather together a range of clothes with zips, toggles, buttons, poppers, fasteners, hooks and Velcro that the children can practise fastening correctly. Ask parents to help with this activity by lending various items for the children to use.

Inform parents of the event and gather as many volunteers as possible.

• • • • • •

Choose a theme.

• • • • • •

Organize a venue.

• • • • • •

Use posters to advertise locally.

• • • • • •

Print tickets and sell them in advance.

• • • • • •

Make decorations with the children.

• • • • • •

Organize refreshments to suit your theme.

• • • • • •

Thank all those involved for their support and inform them of the amount raised.

THEMED COFFEE MORNINGS

What you need
A suitable venue; refreshments; decorations; volunteers; posters; tickets.

Preparation
Decide on a theme for your coffee morning. This could be chosen to tie in with the time of year, a festival or something that the children have been learning about, for example, a daffodil tea, a strawberry tea, a Chinese tea and so on. Organize a venue where tables and chairs can be set out and which has access to a kitchen area. Make posters and advertise the event. Invite the children's families or perhaps residents of local homes for the elderly to attend. Make tickets and set a price. At your group the children could help to make decorations for the event.

Consider whether you could sell something at the coffee morning to help raise funds, for example, punnets of strawberries could be sold at a strawberry tea. As far as possible, try to stick to your theme, even when organizing the snacks. Ask for volunteers for the morning.

What to do
Sell tickets and serve refreshments. Ensure that volunteers keep the area clean and tidy during the event. Run any stalls, sell produce or, if appropriate, lay on your display or entertainment. Volunteers could be dressed to link with the theme, for example, wearing yellow T-shirts for the daffodil tea.

Cups and saucers
Mathematical development
Make four copies of the photocopiable sheet on page 77 and ask a group of four children to colour the cups and saucers on their sheets, matching the cup and saucer pairs in the same colour. If possible, laminate these to extend their lifespan, and cut out the cards. Muddle all the cups and saucers up, then invite the children to match the pairs.

Time of day
Mathematical development
Make a time line with the children to show what happens on a typical day. You could split it into morning, lunchtime, afternoon, teatime and bedtime. Encourage the children to tell you what they do in order to help them to grasp the basic notion of time.

Making decorations
Creative development
Use crêpe paper, tissue, card or other collage materials to make paper flowers as table decorations for the event. The decorations could fit your chosen theme, for example, the children could make red and yellow paper lanterns for a Chinese tea.

CHECKLIST

Inform parents of the event and gather volunteers to be a quiz-master, judges and scorers.

• • • • • •

Write the questions.

• • • • • •

Decide upon a venue, date and time.

• • • • • •

Use posters to advertise locally.

• • • • • •

Write to local community groups, inviting them to enter teams.

• • • • • •

Organize prizes.

• • • • • •

Thank all those involved for their support and inform them of the amount raised.

TEAM QUIZ NIGHT

What you need
Quiz-master; judges and scorers; series of ten rounds of questions; suitable venue; posters; answer sheets; pencils; prizes.

Preparation
You will need to set the quiz, perhaps with ten individual rounds with ten questions in each on topics including sports, history, current affairs, TV and film, food and drink, music and so on. Ensure that the quiz is pitched neither too easy nor too difficult! Prepare numbered answer sheets with the round title, 'Round 3: Sport', and a space for the team name at the top. Invite parents and local community groups or residents to form teams of no more than five people to enter. Charge a fee per team to take part. Organize prizes for the winning team. If this is to be an annual event, you could invest in a small trophy on which the winning team is engraved each year.

What to do
Make sure that the rules have been clearly established as to how long teams have to answer each round and how the rounds will be marked. Ban the use of mobile phones and stress there should be no cheating! Your quiz-master should be someone with a loud clear voice and depending on your venue you may consider using a public address system. Allow the quiz-master to run the event, making sure that the teams know which round they are on and reminding them to put their names on the top of each answer sheet.

After each round, collect in the answers and these should be marked by a team of scorers. At regular intervals the scores should be read out and teams listed in order of score. You might consider providing catering for the evening or teams could be invited to bring their own food and drink as required.

Team problems
Mathematical development

Involve groups of children in simple riddles, puzzles and problems that require them to work together, for example, ask them to find out how many children can stand on one sheet of newspaper or how many children, holding hands, it takes to stretch from one end of your room to the other.

Kid's quiz
Knowledge and understanding of the world

Discuss and explain what the term 'quiz' means. Use the quiz on the photocopiable sheet on page 78 to have fun with the children, seeing which of the questions they can answer.

Working together
Physical development

Develop the children's ability to work together in teams by playing team games in large open spaces. Encourage them to discuss what a team is and how the members of the team can support one another.

CHECKLIST

Inform parents of the event.

• • • • • •

Invite people to enter the show.

• • • • • •

Decide upon a venue, date and time.

• • • • • •

List all the proposed acts.

• • • • • •

Use posters, fliers and local press to advertise.

• • • • • •

Print tickets and sell them in advance.

• • • • • •

Produce programmes.

• • • • • •

Organize compere, video operator and sound technicians.

• • • • • •

Hold a dress rehearsal.

• • • • • •

Issue certificates to recognize everyone's achievements.

• • • • • •

Make a list of people requiring a copy of the video.

• • • • • •

Thank all those involved for their support and inform them of the amount raised.

TALENT SHOW

What you need

Performers; suitable venue; music supply; compère; tickets; posters; video recorder; programmes; certificates; refreshments.

Preparation

Invite people to volunteer an act for the talent show. Include staff, parents, carers, the children and older brothers or sisters. Draw up a list of the proposed acts and create a programme for the show. Set a maximum length for each act and time the show. Each acts will rehearse individually, but it is essential to have at least one full run through of the show so that everyone knows what they are doing. Ask volunteers to be a compère, sound assistant and video operator. Advertise in the local community, using posters, fliers or the local press. Sell tickets both in advance and on the night. Prepare certificates for participants.

What to do

Arrange seats around a performing area and as the audience arrive, sell copies of the programme. Invite the compère to begin the show, introducing each act and saying what they are going to do.

Arrange for the whole show to be videoed and ask the compère to announce at the end that a video of the show will be for sale. Collect names, addresses and monies on the night and arrange for the tapes to be distributed when the copies are ready. Sell refreshments during an interval and award certificates to all those who take part.

Something I'm good at...

Personal, social and emotional development

During a circle time session, encourage the children to tell the others about the things that they feel they have a talent for. This might include swimming, singing, running, listening and so on.

Making tickets

Knowledge and understanding of the world.

Using a computer art package, invite the children to design tickets for the show and to create a front cover for the programme, the text could then be added by an adult. As the children work, talk them through what they are doing, using the correct terms such as 'screen' and 'mouse'.

Sing a song

Creative development

Invite the children to either choose a favourite song or learn a new one with a view to performing it as a group at the show. Alternatively, they could practise a simple dance. Encourage them to work as a group and to think about what the audience will see.

Inform parents of the event and gather s many volunteers as possible.

Decide upon a venue and arrange disco or music.

Use posters and fliers to advertise locally.

Print tickets and sell them in advance.

Arrange prizes if necessary.

Organize refreshments.

Prepare decorations.

Thank all those involved for their support and inform them of the amount raised.

ST VALENTINE'S DISCO

What you need

A disco and disc jockey; suitable venue; posters; tickets; prizes; refreshments; decorations; volunteers.

Preparation

Organize a suitable venue with tables, chairs and room for a dance floor. If the cost of hiring a professional disco is too expensive, use a good portable CD player and ask people to lend a selection of suitable CDs, clearly named so that they can be returned to the correct people. Advertise locally well in advance with posters and fliers and inform parents through a newsletter, inviting them to buy tickets in advance. Enlist volunteers to help set up and decorate your venue and to tidy up at the end of the event.

What to do

Using the theme of St Valentine's Day, consider making relevant decorations such as hearts, cupid-shaped cut-outs and so on. Another idea is to play only songs with the word 'love' in the title. Add to the fun by introducing fancy dress on a specific theme such as 'Hearts and flowers' or 'Famous couples'.

On the day, prepare the venue and ensure that the disc jockey for the evening is there in plenty of time. Provide party snacks and drinks or ask participants to bring their own. Award prizes for the best costume or best dancer.

Circle time
Personal, social and emotional development

Invite the children to share some of the ways in which people show that they love and care for us. Talk about appropriate ways in which other people can demonstrate their love for us.

'I love them because...'
Communication, language and literacy

Encourage the children to think of someone they love such as their mum, dad or sibling and ask them to draw or paint a picture of that person. Ask each child to tell you a reason why they love that person and scribe what they say on to card to display beneath the children's pictures.

Valentine's Day cards
Creative development

Ask an adult to cut some large potatoes in half and to cut a heart shape on the surface of each half. Cut a range of sizes. Let the children use these to make paint prints on to folded card, then ask an adult to help scribe a message from the child inside.

FAMILY HARVEST LUNCH

What you need

A suitable venue, produce stalls; speaker or music; volunteers; posters; tickets; ingredients for a ploughman's lunch.

Preparation

Decide upon a suitable venue which has access to a kitchen area. Arrange a list of volunteers to help prepare and serve the lunches. Invite families and the local community at large to attend, advertising through posters. Charge per ticket to include a ploughman's lunch of cheese, bread, apple, pickle and so on, and aim to sell tickets in advance to make catering easier. Invite local food producers to attend and sell their produce such as pickles, cheeses, jams and so on. These people could be asked to contribute a percentage of their sales or a donation towards the group.

What to do

Purchase food and prepare the lunches, allowing for a few extra people who may wish to join the event on the day. Ask volunteers to serve and tidy up as needed. Organize some soft background music for the venue or invite someone to do a talk, for example, someone could demonstrate how to make corn dollies. Make sure that any guests who are selling their produce have sufficient room and anything else that they might need.

Harvest festivals
Personal, social and emotional development

Talk about harvest festivals and the time of year when these occur. Discuss the importance of giving, sharing and caring for others. Make bread with the children, ask parents to donate bread products on a certain day, and distribute it within the local community such as to a home for the elderly.

All types of bread
Mathematical development

Use some slices of bread to introduce size and shape vocabulary. Talk about thick slices, thin slices, square slices, round slices and rectangular slices. Look at big and small loaves of bread.

Bread around the world
Knowledge and understanding of the world

Look at, touch, taste and smell a variety of bread products from different cultures. Include baguettes, seeded batches, chapatis, naan bread, bagels and croissants. Talk about where these come from and how they might be eaten.

FESTIVAL DECORATIONS EVENING

What you need
Range of craft materials suitable for the chosen crafts; volunteers and demonstrators; posters; tickets; refreshments; a suitable venue.

Preparation
Exploit any artistic talent within your group by asking parents, carers and leaders whether they would be prepared to demonstrate a craft idea to other adults. Choose five or six different ideas for decorations for Christmas or other festivals such as Divali or Chinese New Year, and set up a table for each with all the resources needed. Ideas for Christmas decorations could include salt-dough decorations, chocolate truffles, stockings, Christmas wreaths and so on. Advertise on the group notice-board and by using posters in the wider community. Organize refreshments to serve during the evening.

What to do
Ask each demonstrator to make a sample of the finished articles as an example. Put a demonstrator in charge of each craft table and up to six chairs for interested participants at each. Invite people to either move around all the activities in turn or to choose four of the six to take part in, depending on the time available and the number of interested participants.

Hold a coffee or tea break half-way through the event. At the end of the evening, the participants keep and take home anything that they have made during the event.

Guess the gift
Mathematical development

Invite the children to print or design sheets of wrapping paper and then wrap some regular solid-shaped objects in the paper. Ask the children to name the shape of each object and to guess what the gifts are, for example, a sphere – football, cuboid – video and so on.

Let's celebrate
Knowledge and understanding of the world

Talk about some of the traditions that we have for regular festivals, such as Christmas, and ask if the children know where they have come from. Talk about the tradition of giving gifts. Read a very simple version of the Christmas story, highlighting the gifts given in it, discussing what they are and how this tradition has remained intact after all these years. Remember to emphasize the pleasure of giving as well as receiving. Use the same idea for festivals from other cultures.

Mini Christmas trees
Creative development

Show the children how to make a mini Christmas tree to decorate and use as a table centre-piece. Draw a semicircle with a diameter of approximately 30cm on to thin green card. Let the children cut it out, fold it into a cone shape and tape it together. They can stick green crêpe paper or tissue strips onto it to resemble the branches. Once this is dry, let the children decorate them with small pieces of collage materials.

Everyday fund-raisers

These everyday fund-raising activities can be carried out at any time of the year to suit your setting and own circumstances. Ideas include a sponsored balloon race, a quiz for the family and a cakes and candy sale.

GUESS THE...

What you need

Depends on which activity you choose (see 'What to do' for ideas), for example, 'Guess the birthday' – an unused diary, a soft toy; prize.

Preparation

Place a notice or poster on the wall inviting parents and carers to pay for a guess, perhaps as they deliver or collect their child on a given day.

What to do

This idea requires people to pay to guess a fact, for example, the weight of, number of, birthday of something (cake, sweets in a jar, soft toy).

If you choose to do 'Guess the birthday', set up a table by placing a soft toy and an unused diary beside it where it will catch the eye of parents and carers as they collect their children. Decide on a date, make a record of this and store it carefully. Invite people to pay a fee to write their name beside the date that they think is the toy's birthday. The correct date wins the toy. This activity has the potential to raise 365 times the charge per guess!

Guessing games
Communication, language and literacy

Adapt the game of 'I spy' to a guessing game called 'Guess what I'm thinking of'. Encourage the children to give a description of something in the room, without naming the object. The others take turns at guessing what it is and then they take a turn at describing something.

How many pieces?
Mathematical development

Play estimating games with the children. Keep them simple, for example, place eight pieces of Lego in a tray and ask the children to guess (without counting) how many pieces there are. Count together to check how close each guess was.

Guess the birthday
Knowledge and understanding of the world

Tell the children that a birthday is the anniversary of the day on which they were born and that it is the same date every year. Prepare a chart with the name of each month and an illustration, for example, January (a snowman), February (a Valentine heart) and so on. Using the list, ensure that each child knows the month that they were born. Let the others, in turn, guess which month each child was born in.

BALLOON RACE

What you need

Canister of helium; balloons; string; netting; pre-printed labels; posters; volunteers; prizes.

Preparation

Prepare the labels to provide a space for the name of the person sponsoring the balloon, a space for the name and address of the person who finds the balloon and instruction to return the label to the group's address within 30 days of a specified date. Advertise your balloon race, stating where and when it will be taking place. Invite people to buy labels in advance if they cannot attend on the day. Ask for volunteers.

What to do

On the day of the balloon race, sell labels in advance of the start time. Fill the balloons with helium and knot. Tie a label securely to each balloon and place them under secured netting. At the advertised start time, release the netting, letting the balloons free.

Award prizes to the person whose balloon:

- is returned first
- travelled furthest
- travelled least distance.

You could also award a prize to the person who finds the balloon that travelled furthest as an incentive to send the labels back.

Balloon experiments

Knowledge and understanding of the world

Blow up balloons for the children to work with. (Make sure that the children do not blow them up themselves.) Invite them to rub the balloon along the sleeve of their clothing, then watch what happens if they place the balloon near their hair or a friend's hair. Ask the children what they think causes what they see and discuss possibilities.

Balloon exercises

Physical development

Give each child an air-filled balloon and use these for exercises in a clear, open space. If you wish, play some appropriate music. Ask the children to stretch up high with their balloons or try to keep them from touching the ground. Develop this into a team game with groups of four children each trying to keep their balloons in the air in turn.

Balloon fruit bowl

Creative development

Let the children help you to cover inflated balloons with layers of strips of paper and cellulose paste. Leave to dry. Once hard, cut the cast in half to form a bowl shape. Invite the children to decorate their bowl, then cover with PVA glue to create a fruit bowl.

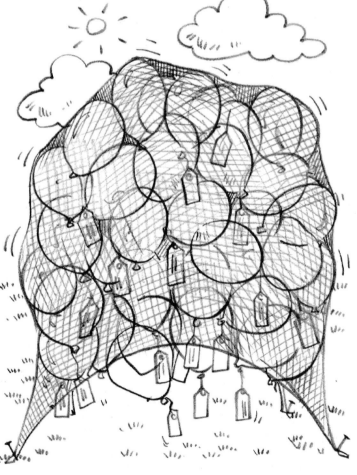

CHECKLIST

Inform parents of the event.

● ● ● ● ● ●

Identify an adjudicator and give their name on the quiz letter.

● ● ● ● ● ●

Use posters to advertise locally.

● ● ● ● ● ●

Decide upon a return date for completed quiz sheets.

● ● ● ● ● ●

Make copies of the quiz and letter.

● ● ● ● ● ●

Organize a prize.

● ● ● ● ● ●

Arrange to sell the quiz sheet through shops.

● ● ● ● ● ●

Mark all quiz sheets and notify winner.

● ● ● ● ● ●

Thank all those involved for their support and inform them of the amount raised.

FAMILY FAVOURITES QUIZ

What you need
The photocopiable sheet on page 79; answers on page 62; volunteer to be adjudicator; posters; prize.

Preparation
Find a volunteer, whose details can be put on the reverse of the quiz sheet, to act as marker and adjudicator. Make and display posters advertising the event. Make as many copies of the quiz as you think you can sell. Add a covering slip to the quiz sheet explaining the procedures, for example: These clues all relate to something from the world of children's entertainment including books, films and TV. Some of the clues are straightforward, some will tax your memory and some are cryptic! On completion, this form should be sent to (named contact or address) for marking no later than (finish date). In the event of a tie, the winning form will be drawn from a hat. Winners will be informed by (however). Thank you for your support. The proceeds from this quiz sheet are going towards (specific reason for fund-raising).

Ask local shops if they will sell the quiz on your behalf. Obtain a prize. Set the return date far enough in advance to give you time to sell a good number of the quiz sheets.

What to do
Give each child and adult in the group a number of quiz sheets (perhaps ten) to try to sell. Ask them to return any monies or unsold sheets by a set date. Place copies of the quiz in as many local establishments as possible – pubs, schools, library and so on if they are willing to collect the money for them.

Completed sheets should all be sent to an adjudicator who has the answers. Arrange for the sheets to be marked as they arrive and the total score recorded on the front. The highest score is the winner. In the event of a tie, place all 'winners' in a hat and draw an overall winner. Display the answer sheet on your notice-board for interested participants.

Favourite programme graph
Mathematical development
Make a graph to show the children's favourite television programmes. Limit the choice to four or five programmes, place a picture of the characters from each option along the bottom of the graph and write the corresponding children's names in a column above. Ask the children simple questions such as 'Which programme was liked by most children?'.

Finding out
Knowledge and understanding of the world
Ask the children to find out from their parents what their own favourite characters were when they were young. Invite parents to come into a session to show some of their old books, comics, toy figures or videos.

Character collage
Creative development
Provide a range of materials for the children to create a collage of their favourite character. Encourage them to discuss what kind of material would best suit a particular area, for example, wool for Elmer's tail.

FILL A TUBE

What you need

A tube of sweets, such as Smarties, for each child; a note to attach to each tube; poster.

Preparation

You need to decide whether to give the children empty tubes, or let them have the sweets at home. The cost of the sweets will have to be deducted from your total raised, unless you can buy them as snack for a session and write the cost off against your snack fund. Consider any child who may have an allergy or dietary requirement, and may be unable to eat the sweets.

Prepare a note aimed at the child such as 'Please enjoy these sweets and when they are finished, keep the tube. Can you fill it with as many coins as possible and return it to our group by (give date)? Thank you.'

What to do

Attach a copy of the note to each tube of sweets and give a tube to each child. Display a poster on the notice-board reminding parents and carers of the date the tubes should be returned by.

Which coins fit?

Mathematical development

Let the children use plastic coins to see which ones will fit into the sweets tube. Put the coins into piles – those that fit and those that will not. Provide a range of other empty tubes and ask the children to find one that all coins would fit into.

Tubes and tunnels

Physical development

Provide a range of tubes or tunnels in a clear, open space for the children to crawl through. Use plastic, manufactured play tunnels if you have access to them, if not, the children can form tunnels with their bodies, by placing hands and feet on the ground and forming an arch, side by side. Ask them to find different ways of moving through the tunnels – can they wriggle, slither and so on?

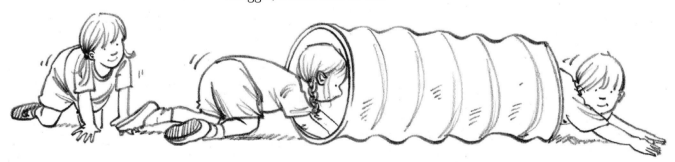

Three-dimensional junk modelling

Creative development

Provide a range of 3-D junk for modelling and discuss the shapes with the children. Ask them to point out items that are the same kind of shape as the tube that they have been asked to fill. Try to gather as many tubes or cylinders as possible and encourage the children to use these to make junk models.

WHICH HOLIDAY DESTINATION?

What you need
Large map of the United Kingdom; notice; cocktail sticks; sticky labels; Blu-Tack; prize.

Preparation
Obtain a large map of the United Kingdom that is not too detailed. Use a highlighter pen to mark a selection of locations, including one that you have chosen as the 'winning destination'. Keep a written note of the chosen place in a secret location. Prepare flags by wrapping strips of sticky labels around cocktail sticks. Prepare a notice explaining the activity and what the prize will be.

What to do
Engage the children's interest by telling them that this year Teddy (choose one from your toy-box) went on holiday. Invite the people to guess where he went. Display the map and notice in a prominent position. Charge people to write their name on to a flag and stick it, with Blu-Tack, if necessary, on to the map where they think Teddy went. If there are a few locations close together that would make the winner difficult to determine, ask them to write the name of their chosen location onto the flag as well.

Once all the destinations have been selected, reveal the secret destination and notify the winner. Post the details on the notice-board in order to keep everyone informed, and to thank them for taking part.

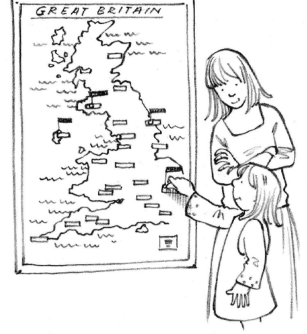

Travel agency
Communication, language and literacy
Set up a travel agency in the role-play area. Obtain old posters and brochures from a local travel agent and provide seats, a telephone, paper, pencils and, if possible, a computer monitor (made from a box) and keyboard. Encourage the children to take turns to pretend to be the travel agent and the customer.

Postcards
Communication, language and literacy
Invite the children to look at and discuss real postcards. Encourage them to talk about any holidays that they have had or any interesting places that they have visited. Support the children in making postcards for a place that they have visited and display these alongside a scribed sentence or two describing their destination.

Pack your case
Physical development
Give each child a large cut-out paper or card suitcase shape. Provide a selection of old magazines or catalogues and encourage the children to cut out pictures of items that they would take on holiday with them. Invite the children to stick these on to the suitcase shape. Encourage the children to explain why they have chosen each item as they work through the activity.

SCAVENGER HUNT

What you need
Copies of the hunt list; prize; posters.

Preparation
Consider your local environment and make a list of things that you wish teams to find. Ideas might include a daisym different types of leaves, a timetable from the local leisure centre, a plastic bag from a local shop and so on. Confirm with shops or leisure centres that they are willing to support the hunt. Have one or two special tie-breaker items which would be difficult, but not impossible, to find. Roughly time the hunt and set the time limit accordingly. Invite parents and relatives to participate with their children. Use posters to advertise throughout the local community.

What to do
Be at the designated point well before the start time of the event. Participants pay for a copy of the scavenger list and should be told the finish time and place (if different from start). Emphasize that anyone turning up late will not have their collection checked. When the start time arrives, let the teams begin. The winner is the team with the most listed items returning within the given time.

Puzzles and problems
Mathematical development
Present the children with simple mathematical problems using the items found on the scavenger hunt, for example, 'Can you make a play-dough caterpillar that is too big to fit on to the leaf?'; 'Sort these things into different sets – natural and manufactured or by colours'; 'Stick three feathers into this Blu-Tack' and so on.

Leaf art
Knowledge and understanding of the world
Look at the leaves that were collected on the hunt. Discuss how they differ from each other or any similarities that they have. Use some of them to make crayon rubbings and others to make prints with by painting the leaves, laying paper over them and then gently pressing to make a print. Observe the veins of the leaves and look at human veins on the children's arms in comparison. Discuss, at a simple level, the similarity of their functions.

Hunt collage
Creative development
Make a collage to represent your community by sticking the items that the children and their families have collected during the hunt on to a large piece of frieze paper. You could ask the children to sort the items first, then group together things of a similar nature.

CHECKLIST
Inform parents of the event and ask them to send in cakes and sweets.

• • • • • •

Liaise with local primary school, if appropriate.

• • • • • •

Use posters to advertise.

• • • • • •

Thank parents and inform them of the amount raised.

CAKES AND CANDY

What you need
Donations of cakes and sweets; posters; food bags, cling film or similar.

Preparation
Inform parents, carers and staff well in advance so that they have time to donate things (home-made or bought) to sell. Involve the children in making cakes and sweets during their sessions, which could also be sold. They could also be involved in counting the cakes and wrapping them in bags of two, four or six. Remember to highlight the importance of washing hands thoroughly before baking or handling foodstuff.

What to do
Inform parents of when you intend selling the cakes and sweets and arrange a time when they can come in to buy items. Encourage them to tell friends, family and neighbours. You could also arrange with your local primary school to sell some of the products at break time. Give them plenty of notice so that the children are reminded to bring money to school with them on the appropriate day.

New foods
Personal, social and emotional development
Discuss trying new foods. Ask the children to talk about what they like to eat. Encourage them to think of something new that they have tasted and liked and something new that they didn't like. Try to highlight the fact that you cannot say you dislike something you have never even tried!

Describe it!
Communication, language and literacy
Cut photographs of cakes and sweets from old magazines or off product labels and stick them onto squares of card. Play a game where one child describes the item on the card by shape, size and colour and the other children have to guess which one item is being described.

Five currant buns
Mathematical development
Develop the children's knowledge of number with this rhyme.
> 'Five currant buns in a baker's shop,
> Round and fat with sugar on the top,
> Along came (child's name) with a penny one day,
> Bought a currant bun and took it away.
> Four currant buns in a baker's shop…'.
> The children can line up as currant buns and other children could be the individuals 'buying' them and taking them away.

TREASURE MAP

What you need
Large sheet of paper; prize or prizes; posters; volunteers.

Preparation
On a large sheet of paper, draw a rectangle or square, leaving room along the sides to insert letters and numbers as co-ordinates for each square. Carefully draw grid lines. (A square of side 80cm, split into 5cm squares, will result in 256 squares.) Ask anyone artistic in the group to draw, within your shape, a treasure island. Obtain a prize or prizes depending on how many squares you have on the map. Choose the winning squares and keep a record in a safe place.

What to do
The aim is to 'sell' each square on the grid. You are unlikely to sell all the squares within your group, so arrange with a local supermarket to set up a table at their entrance. Draw up a rota for volunteers to man the table. People pay to write their name and contact number within the square where they believe the treasure is hidden. Display a poster explaining who you are, why you are fund-raising and what the prizes are.

Cover the map with adhesive plastic so that you can use it again and prepare a sheet with all the co-ordinates marked on which people write on, or use non-permanent markers on the plastic coating.

Co-ordinates games
Mathematical development
Make up simple co-ordinate games and activities using colours and numbers to ten as the reference points. Using the map on the photocopiable sheet on page 80, colour in a different colour in each of the boxes along the bottom. Ask the children to place little 'treasures' into a given square, for example, blue 4. Other children must then try to find the treasure from a given reference. On a larger scale, draw a grid, in chalk, on the ground. Call out a reference and ask the children to stand in that square.

Bird's eye view
Knowledge and understanding of the world
Explain that maps show objects as they would appear from above. If possible, show a simple example of this. Let the children take photographs of everyday items, from above, then invite other children try to guess what the objects are.

Treasure maps
Creative development
Give each child a copy of the photocopiable sheet on page 80. Discuss pirates and buried treasure with the children. Let them 'age' their copies of the map by scrunching it up and giving it a 'wash' using an old, damp tea-bag. Once they are dry, encourage the children to draw on them with felt-tipped pens, adding treasure and other details.

CHECKLIST

Inform parents of the event.

Prepare pictures and answer sheet.

Contact a variety of local establishments to display the pictures.

Use posters and the local press to advertise.

Organize a prize.

Thank everyone involved for their support, circulate answers and inform them of the winner and the amount raised.

PICTURE HUNT

What you need
Laminated A4 pictures; picture list answer sheet; posters; prize.

Preparation
Draw and colour pictures related to your current theme on pieces of A4 card, for example, if your theme is 'The seaside' draw a crab, a shell, a fish and so on. You will need between ten to 15 pictures which should be numbered in the top right-hand corner. Prepare an answer sheet with space for the name and contact address or telephone number of the participant and the numbers for however many pictures down the side. You need to place these pictures around the local area, liaising with shops, the library, the church, residents and so on, asking if they will place a picture in their windows. Make a note of where each picture is displayed. Organize a prize for the winner.

What to do
Advertise your picture hunt both within the group and the wider community. Charge participants for an answer sheet and invite them to find the pictures in the local area, writing the locations alongside the corresponding number on the sheet. Encourage parents to involve their children as much as possible on the picture hunt. Give a closing date and address for completed sheets. The winner is the person who correctly identifies the location of all the pictures. If there is more than one winner, draw the winning name from a box.

Picture hunt story
Communication, language and literacy
Read the story 'The picture hunt' on the photocopiable sheet on page 64 about two children who look for pictures in their town on a picture hunt. It may be a good idea to read the story just before the picture hunt, as it will explain the activity to the children and should inspire them to take part.

Computer artwork
Knowledge and understanding of the world
Let the children use a drawing program on the computer to make designs for some of the pictures to be used in the hunt.

Object hunt
Physical development
Hide a number of familiar items around the room, for example, building blocks. Tell the children how many you have hidden and ask them to try to find them. They might be under, above, behind or inside other items. As the children search, encourage them by saying 'Hotter...hotter' as they get near, or 'Colder...colder' as they get further away.

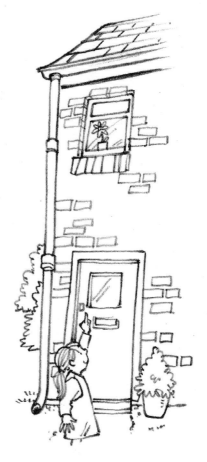

BUY A BRICK

What you need

Frieze paper; paper brick shapes; display area; posters.

Preparation

Cut a selection of brick shapes from stiff paper. Clear a prominent wall space to display your frieze or, better still, arrange for the finished piece to be displayed within a community building such as at the local primary school or in a village or community hall.

What to do

Advertise your 'Buy a brick' scheme in the local press, stating your aim to build a wall of messages of friendship, love and achievement. Explain that people can buy a card brick and place photos of friends or children, messages, poems and so on, for someone special, on to them. Also highlight what you hope to achieve with the money raised, and where the finished 'wall' will be displayed.

Sell the 'bricks' through your group, shops or community venues such as the library, if possible. Adult volunteers may be willing to go round homes, in pairs. Give people a drop off point for completed bricks and use them to 'build a wall' by sticking them to the frieze paper.

Investigating bricks
Communication, language and literacy

Provide the children with a variety of real bricks and ask them to carefully hold and feel them. Encourage the children to think of words to describe them – heavy, hard, rough and so on. Invite a local builder in to talk to the children, showing them how bricks are stuck together and how walls are built. Ask the builder to talk about safety on the building site and to bring in a real hard hat and some of his tools. Encourage the children to ask questions and listen carefully.

Building walls
Physical development

Make 'bricks' using empty cardboard packaging painted or covered with appropriately-coloured paper. Let the children build walls with these, using glue as mortar. Once dry, test out the walls to see how sturdy they are and look at which designs worked best.

Humpty Dumpty
Creative development

Sing the nursery rhyme 'Humpty Dumpty' with the children. Use rectangular sponges and paint to print a wall and make a collage of Humpty to 'sit' on it. You could also perform the nursery rhyme, nominating a Humpty and the King's men.

Useful addresses and contacts

Suppliers of fund-raising materials

These companies may be able to support the fund-raising activities described in Chapter 4. In addition, there are contact details for companies that may supply materials to make fairs, fêtes and social events a great success.

All My Own Work

The Cottage, Town End Road, Draycott, DERBY DE72 3PT
Tel: 01332 875719
Fax: 01332 874072

All My Own Work provide ideas to be creative, have fun and raise funds at the same time. They provide a range of fund-raising projects that allow the children to have their work made into a range of eye-catching and useful products to sell to raise funds for your group. Ideas include gym bags, placemats and teddies.

Baker Ross Limited

Unit 53, Millmead Industrial Estate, Mill Mead Road, LONDON N17 9QU
Tel: 020 8808 2663
Fax: 020 8801 1611
www.bakerross.co.uk

The Baker Ross catalogue includes a large selection of money-making and entertaining ideas for fund-raising events. These include tombolas, stall packs and games.

Chris Aston Ceramics

4 High Street, Elkesley, NOTTINGHAM DN22 8AJ
Tel: 01777 838391
www.chrisastonceramics.co.uk

Chris Aston Ceramics specializes in the production of screen-printed enamel decoration on mugs and plates. These mugs can be used for fund-raising, anniversaries or end of year leaving presentations.

Electronic Clothing

Unit 1, Bessemer Park, Bessemer Road, BASINGSTOKE RG21 3NB
Tel: 0800 9809494
www.teatowel.com

Electronic Clothing's brochure covers a range of fund-raising products which include book bags, shoe bags, tea towels, sun-hats, mugs and painting overalls.

Ha'penny Press

Caxton House, Holbrook, IPSWICH IP9 2QS
Tel: 01473 328400
www.raffle.co.uk

Ha'penny Press supplies millions of draw tickets to UK charities and the printing trade. Contact them for a free copy of their brochure.

Happyhands

55 Sloane Square, LONDON SW1 8AX
Tel: 020 7730 5544
www.ontiles.com

Happyhands capture early childhood in a unique and personal way. A range of their products include children's handprints and footprints on ceramics; first works of art and kiss tiles. These could be sold to parents and carers in your group as a fund-raising event.

Partybox.co.uk

3 Midsummer Walk, WOKING GU21 4RG
Tel: 01483 755346
www.partybox.co.uk

Order a complete party in a box from Partybox.co.uk. There are hundreds of products including over 60 tableware themes. Included on their website is a directory to other websites that can help you locate anything from music for children's parties to bouncy castles and marquees.

Peeks of Bournemouth Limited
Reid Street, Fairmile Road,
Christchurch, DORSET BH23 2BT
Tel: 01202 489449
www.peeks.co.uk

Peeks produce a fund-raising catalogue packed withticket games, side-show games and printed balloons as well as a complete range of bunting, flags, banners and event accessories. They offer a 'Theme range', with thousands of decorations and novelties to cover themes such as St Valentine's Day, Mexican and Rock 'n' Roll.

Permark Name Tapes
Permark House, 4 Lavender Gardens, HARROW WEALD HA3 6DD
Tel: 020 8954 6333
www.nametapesdirect.com

Permark supply name tapes, name tags, clothing labels and luggage straps. This may be a worthwhile fund-raiser just before the children leave your group to go to school, so that they have labels for their school uniform, PE kit and so on.

Pictureproducts
PO Box 9, Snodland, KENT ME6 5LW
Tel: 01634 243450
Fax: 01634 242885

'Memories that last for ever' – Pictureproducts reproduce children's drawings or

photographs onto high quality melamine plates or clocks. The company provides an organizer's pack that gives six easy steps to organizing this type of fund-raising event.

Sound Sense
Tel: 020 7687 0445
www.soundsensecd.co.uk

Sound Sense offer a complete service to produce the children's own CD including recording, editing, artwork and printing as well as CD duplication.

Stuart Morris Textiles
Riverside Print House, Pound Lane HADLEIGH IP7 5EQ
Tel: 0800 7311273
www.schoolteatowel.com

Stuart Morris Textiles produce a wide range of fund-raising merchandise that includes tea towels, mugs, calendars, paperweights, bags, aprons, and caps.

Webb Ivory
PRESTON PR0 2QX
Tel: 0870 605 5000

Webb Ivory Christmas Fund-raising catalogues contain pages of festive cards, wrap and gifts. These catalogues can be distributed to friends and family of your group to do some of their Christmas shopping.

Party plan organizations

Host a party at your setting with one of these party plan companies. All you have to do is book the party, invite guests and the demonstrator will do the rest.

Tupperware UK & Ireland
Keaton House, Widewater Place, Moorhall Road, Harefield, Uxbridge, MIDDLESEX UB9 6NS
Tel:01895 826400
www.tupperware.co.uk

PartyLite UK Limited
Monument House, 215 Marsh Road, Pinner, MIDDLESEX HA5 5NE
Tel: 02083856600
www.partylite.co.uk

The Body Shop
Tel: 08459 050607
www.thebodyshop.co.uk

Interested organizations

Within this section are a range of government and non-government organizations that provide a range of support services for those involved in fund-raising.

Charities Aid Foundation
Head Office, Kings Hill Avenue, Kings Hill, WEST MALLING ME19 4TA
Tel: 01732 520000
www.cafonline.org

The Charities Aid Foundation's unique purpose is to provide support for non-government organizations. A range of helpful information sheets can be accessed through their website. They publish a range of useful books on fund-raising and applying to grant making trusts.

Charity Commission for England and Wales
Harmsworth House, 13–15 Bouverie Street, LONDON EC4Y 8DP
General Enquiries Line
Tel: 0870 333 0123
www.charity-commission.gov.uk
This government organization keeps an up-to-date register of

all the charities currently listed in the United Kingdom. Responsibility also lies with them for legislation surrounding charities and charitable events. They produce a range of helpful literature including 'Charities and Fund-raising' (CC20) and 'Providing Alcohol on Charity Premises' (CC27).

Directory of Social Change
24 Stephenson Way, LONDON
NW1 2DP
Tel: 0207 209 4949
www.dsc.org.uk

The DSC was set up in 1975 to help voluntary and community organizations become more effective. Areas of expertise include helping voluntary groups to raise the money they need and to plan and develop for the future.

Gaming Board for Great Britain
Berkshire House, 168–173 High Holburn, LONDON WC1V 7AA
Tel: 020 7306 6200
www.gbgb.org.uk

The Gaming Board can help you make sure that you are not breaking any rules, particularly relating to raffles and lotteries. They produce a helpful document called 'Lotteries and the Law'.

National Council for Voluntary Organizations
Regent's Wharf, 8 All Saints Street, LONDON N1 9RL
Tel: 0800 279 8798
www.ncvo-vol.org.uk

The NCVO provide information, training funding opportunities and services for voluntary groups. Their legal team can provide legal advice on charity law and legal structures.

Performing Right Society
29–33 Berners Street,
LONDON
W1T 3AB
Tel: 020 7580 5544

Performing Right Society
3 Rothesay Place,
EDINBURGH
EH3 7SL
Tel: 0131 242 5713
www.prs.co.uk

The Performing Right Society grant licenses the use of music for specific premises. Schools are often covered for this through their local authority, however, it may be worthwhile contacting the PRS to verify that your premises are licensed.

Scottish Council for Voluntary Organizations
Tel: 0131 556 3882 (Edinburgh)
0141 332 5660 (Glasgow)
01463 235633 (Inverness).
www.scvo.org.uk

This is the umbrella group for voluntary organizations in Scotland, with offices in Edinburgh, Glasgow and Inverness. This is a sister organization to the NCVO in England. Sister councils in Wales and Ireland are the Wales Council for Voluntary Action and the Northern Ireland Council for Voluntary Action.

Trading Standards Central
www.tradingstandards.gov.uk

This website will give you the details of your local trading standards office who can advise you about selling second-hand goods. This website also provides additional information to fund-raisers.

Publications and websites
These organizations and websites can provide helpful information about fund-raising.

DfES Publications
PO Box 5050, Sherwood Park,
Annesley, NOTTINGHAM
NG15 0DJ
Tel: 0845 6022260
Fax: 0845 6033360
www.dfes.gov.uk

As part of the DfES's Good Practice in Childcare series there is a title called *A Guide to Fund-raising*. The booklet has been written by the Kid's Clubs Network and includes chapters on planning your fund-raising, organizing events and charitable trusts and foundations. Copies can be downloaded from the internet at www.dfee.gov.uk/eydcp

National Confederation of Parent Teacher Associations
18 St Johns Hill, Sevenoaks, KENT
TN13 3NP
Tel: 01732 748850
www.ncpta.org.uk

NCPTA promotes partnerships between home and school; pupils, parents, carers and teachers; parents and local education authorities and other interested organizations. Membership of this

confederation automatically provides insurance cover and protection for PTA events.
The NCPTA publish *Home and School*, a termly magazine with regular sections on fund-raising.

Pre-School Learning Alliance

69 Kings Cross Road,
LONDON
WC1X 9LL
Tel: 020 7833 0991
www.pre-school.org.uk

The Pre-School Learning Alliance publish a fund-raising pack intended to help pre-school groups raise money. The pack is made up of a number of fact sheets covering a range of topics from applying to trusts to planning fund-raising activities.

Fund-raising for Small Groups Newsletter

www.fund-raising-newsletters.com/small.html

This free monthly newsletter sent by email is for groups that mainly rely on product fund-raising and sometimes hold events to raise money. The 'Fund-raising for Small Groups Newsletter' comes to you monthly with tips, tricks, suggestions, secrets and resources that you can use to improve your fund-raising abilities and success.

Fund-Raising.com

www.fund-raising.com
This is an American-based website which has an extensive bank of fund-raising ideas.

As internet shopping becomes

more popular, certain shopping outlets are trying to help schools and early years groups raise funds. Listed below are three of these companies.

SchoolKitty

www.SchoolKitty.co.uk

SchoolKitty is a UK-based website dedicated to harnessing the power of the Internet to provide a simple way for parents, friends and family, in fact anyone with access to the Web, to help raise funds for the school of their choice just by shopping online. Importantly, the funds raised are forwarded to the school at the beginning of each term as a lump sum. Each participating school can therefore spend its 'SchoolKitty pot' on the resources that it really needs such as books, computers, sports equipment, or whatever they want.

go-help

www.go-help.co.uk

go-help is all about allowing you to make money for the good cause – school, charity or club – of your choice from your Internet shopping. And you pay no more for your shopping than you would if you'd gone directly to the stores.

Schoolboost.com

www.schoolboost.com

Schoolboost.com is a way of helping you to raise money for the school you care about without incurring any extra costs to you or the school. Simply register with Schoolboost.com and when you make an online purchase at any of our hundreds of affiliated retailers a percentage of your purchases will directly benefit your chosen school.

Charitable trusts, foundations and other grant-making organizations

Many charitable trusts and foundations give money to organizations that are delivering services to young children. Here are some of these trusts and foundations.

The Directory of Social Change

(page 59) publish guides to local trusts: Volume 1 North; Volume 2 Midlands; Volume 3 London; Volume 4 South.
The Charities Aid Foundation (page 58) publish *The Directory of Grant Making Trusts Focus Series: Children and Youth* and *Applying to a Grant Making Trust*.

Awards for All Lottery Grants

Awards for All Headquarters,
9th Floor, Camelford House,
89 Albert, Embankment, LONDON
SE1 7UF
Tel: 0207 7587 6600
www.awardsforall.org.uk

Awards for All distributes lottery money to support schools and community groups. The main aim of the programme is to fund projects which involve people in their community; bringing them together to enjoy arts, sports, heritage and other community activities. The headquarters of Awards for All will help you to locate your nearest office.

BBC Children in Need
PO Box 76, LONDON W3 6FS
Tel: 0208 576 7788
www.bbc.co.uk/cin/charity/grants

Grants are made to self-help groups, voluntary organizations and registered charities working with children who are disadvantaged.

Calouste Gulbenkian Foundation
UK Branch, 98 Portland Place, LONDON W1N 4ET
Tel: 020 7636 5313
www.gulbenkian.org.uk

Applications are invited from pre-school groups to support projects specifically established for the purpose of promoting the emotional well-being of pre-school children.

Esmee Fairbairn Foundation
11 Park Place, LONDON SW1A 1LP
Tel: 020 7297 4700
www.esmeefairbairn.org.uk

The Esmee Fairbairn Foundation welcomes a broad range of applications but gives priority to specific areas including early years development covering the years 0–5. They are particularly interested in partnerships between early education providers and other agencies with clear benefits for pre-school children and the wider community; professional development opportunities that will enhance high-quality play and learning activities in non-

statutory early years settings and improving access to pre-school education for children with physical or learning disabilities.

Vicky Hurst Trust
33 Hugh Street, LONDON SW1V 1QJ
Tel: 020 7828 2844
This trust gives grants of up to £1000 to fund projects that will improve the care and education of groups of children under the age of eight. The trust was set up in 1998 after the death of Vicky Hurst who was a nursery school teacher and Chair of the National Campaign for Nursery Education.

Other children's charities
These three charities help children throughout the United Kingdom with specific needs. Organizing a fund-raising event to benefit one of these charities adds to the personal, social and emotional development programme within your group as well as helping to develop the children's sense of citizenship. Links with outside agencies could be formed – perhaps a representative from the chosen charity would be willing to come and talk to the children or thank them and present them with badges and stickers. It is advisable to carry out a search on the Internet or look in your local Yellow Pages for further relevant charities, for example, if a child has a hearing impairment in the group, you may want to develop relationships with a local hearing impairment charity.

Make-a-Wish
Make-a-Wish House, Minster Court, Tuscam

Way, CAMBERLEY GU15 3YY
Tel: 01276 24127
www.make-a-wish.org.uk

The sole aim of this charity is granting wishes of children aged between three and 18 suffering from life-threatening illnesses. Children's fantasies can truly be turned into realities.

Barnardo's
Tanners Lane, Barkingside, Ilford, ESSEX IG6 1QG
Tel: 020 8550 8822
www.barnardos.org.uk/Events/bigtoddle/index.htm

The Big Toddle for Barnardo's is a special fund-raising event for children under five which takes place every summer. Participating groups keep 25% of what they raise for their own group.

DiabetesUK
Central Office, 10 Queen Anne Street, LONDON W1G 9LH
Tel: 020 7323 1531
www.diabetes.org.uk/get/commun/denimn.htm

Diabetes UK run a 'Denim for Diabetes' for groups to heighten children's awareness of diabetes and raise funds for children with diabetes. They produce education packs that can be ordered on the website.

Answers to quizzes on pages 78 and 79.

• • • • • • CHILDREN'S QUIZ • • • • • •

1	Little Miss Muffet	9	Jess
2	Doodles	10	One
3	Seven	11	Three
4	Po	12	Red
5	Mr Tickle	13	An egg
6	Fly	14	Noah
7	Bob the Builder	15	Pinnochio
8	To fetch a pail of water		

• • • • • • FAMILY FAVOURITES QUIZ • • • • • •

1	Ringo Starr	17	Fantasia
2	Thelma and Daphne	18	Happy, Sleepy, Grumpy, Sneezy, Dopey, Bashful and Doc
3	Bob the Builder		
4	Friday, five to five	19	Byker Grove
5	Scar	20	George, Zippy, Bungle and Jeffrey
6	Bill and Ben	21	Muffin the Mule
7	Greyskull	22	Steamboat Willie
8	Noughts and crosses	23	Doodles
9	The Herb Garden	24	Dudley Dursley
10	A vacuum cleaner	25	A hare
11	Dumbo	26	1800 mph
12	Alastair	27	Grange Hill
13	Mr Lazy	28	Fingerbobs
14	Kenneth Williams	29	An orang-utan
15	Robin Williams	30	Big Friendly Giant
16	Brian		

The broken promise

Amy and Adam were twins, but they were very different from each other. Adam had fair hair, and Amy had brown. Adam liked playing with his trains and cars, but Amy enjoyed drawing and colouring.

One day, when they were shopping with Mummy, they both wanted to help in different ways.

'Can I push the trolley, please?' shouted Adam.

'And I'll help you find things,' said Amy.

Because they had been so helpful, Mummy said she would buy them some sweets.

Adam chose fruit gums, which he said he would eat when he got home, but Amy decided to have chocolate buttons to eat in the car.

Sitting on the back seat, Amy started to eat her sweets.

'Can I have one, please?' asked Adam.

Amy held out the packet, but Adam took several buttons from the pack.

'No!' shouted Amy. 'Only one – you have your fruit gums to eat, these are mine!'

'But my gums are packed away now, and I feel hungry. Plea...se!' said Adam. 'If you share your chocolate buttons, *I promise* I will share my fruit gums when we get home.'

'All right – but don't forget!' said Amy sharing the buttons between them.

When they arrived home, Amy rushed inside to finish a picture she had been colouring. Later, after tea, she remembered the fruit gums, and asked Adam for her share.

'I've eaten them!' said Adam

'But you promised to share them with me!' Amy said.

'Too late now, they've all gone!' said Adam, and ran off to his room, laughing.

Amy was upset, because she had trusted Adam, and now she felt he had tricked her.

The next day, the twin's grandma came to see them, and brought them each a lovely picture book. Amy's book had some super pictures of cars and trains in it and although Adam liked his own book, he wanted to see those pictures in Amy's book.

'If you let me borrow your book,' he said, 'I *promise* I will let you borrow mine.'

'But that's what you said about the fruit gums,' said Amy, thoughtfully. 'And you didn't keep your promise did you?'

'Well I will this time. I *promise*!' said Adam.

But Amy wasn't sure she could trust Adam again. What do you think she should do?

Brenda Williams

The picture hunt

Kristian woke up, jumped out of bed and threw open his curtains. Hooray! It was a lovely, sunny morning, which meant that he, his little sister, Daisy, and his mummy would go on the picture hunt today. Kristian's play leaders had hidden ten seaside pictures all around Littlehill, where Kristian lived, and now he had to try to find them.

Kristian couldn't wait to get started. He dressed twice as quickly as usual, ate breakfast twice as quickly as usual and brushed his hair twice as quickly as usual. Then he waited impatiently for Mummy. At last it was time to go. Mummy took the list of pictures, grabbed Daisy's buggy and they set off.

'Let's start at my nursery,' said Kristian.

'That's a good idea,' said Mummy. When they reached nursery, Kristian walked slowly round the outside.

'Mummy, look!' he cried, pointing to a picture of a fish in one of the windows. 'Well done,' said Mummy. She wrote 'nursery' opposite 'fish' on the answer sheet.

Next, they headed towards the newsagent's and looked carefully in the window. There were posters, notices, advertisements and.. a picture of a shell!

The hunt continued. They found a picture of a sandcastle at the library, a crab at the station and a boat in the post office.

'We've found five now!' Kristian shouted.

Mummy decided that they should have a break and some juice. As they reached the café, Daisy began to point and say 'star' excitedly.

'Oh look,' said Mummy. 'Daisy's found the starfish!'

'Good girl!' said Kristian.

After a short rest, their search began again. They found three more pictures, however they just could not find the last one – a shark – anywhere. Finally, Mummy said they should go home.

Kristian was very disappointed. He'd wanted to find all ten pictures. He trudged sadly behind Mummy until they reached their gate.

'Kristian, look!' said Daisy.

'No,' he said grumpily.

'I think you should,' said Mummy. Kristian looked up and there, on Daisy's bedroom window, was the shark. He was overjoyed! Mummy had agreed to put a picture in their window because they lived on the main street. The search had ended much closer to home than Kristian could ever have imagined!

Susan Smith

A hand to touch

A hand to touch
A hand to fold
A hand to make
A hand to mould
A hand to help
A hand to hold.

Brenda Williams

These feet

These feet will walk
a million miles!
Let every step
bring happy smiles!

Brenda Williams

Things to do at the fun-fair!

Paint bright colours on your face.   *(mime painting face)*

Loose balloons, to blow and race.   *(throw arm upwards as though releasing a balloon)*

Throw a sponge at Aunty Jane.   *(look determined and mime throwing forwards)*

Try a lucky dip – again!   *(close eyes and pretend to search a barrel with one hand)*

Cheer your team at tug o' war.   *(look excited and wave an imaginary rattle)*

Sip a milkshake through a straw.   *(mime sipping a straw)*

Roll a penny. Race and run.   *(draw rolling circles in the air)*

Just join in – it's lots of fun!   *(run on the spot)*

Brenda Williams

The graduation song

Some of our friends must leave to-day, Leave to-day, leave to-day.

Some of our friends must leave to-day. It's time to wave good-bye now.

2. We have had lots of fun and games,
Fun and games, fun and games.
We have had lots of fun and games,
It's time to wave 'goodbye' now.

(children who are not leaving stand in a group and sing, 'leavers' walk on and join them)

(children clap as they sing and wave for the last line)

3. Remember playing with water,
With water, with water,
Remember playing with water,
It's time to wave 'goodbye' now.

(all children pretend to splash in the water, before waving for the last line)

4. We hope you have fun at 'big school',
At 'big school', at 'big school'.
We hope you have fun at 'big school',
It's time to wave 'goodbye' now.

(as children sing, the 'leavers' walk away from the group while the other children and staff wave and shout 'goodbye')

Sally Scott

My bag of sounds

My bag of sounds

Shape scene

My book

1. Fold along the lines and cut the book out

2.
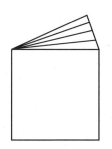

3.

4.
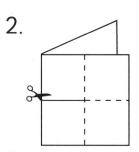

5.
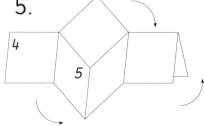

6.
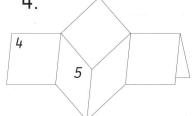

Enlarge outline to approximately A4 size.

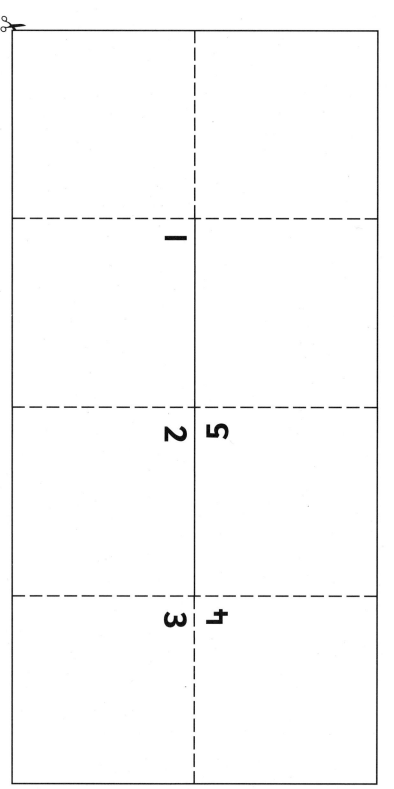

Animal snap

Christmas hamper

Please sign against an item(s) that you are willing to contribute to our Christmas hamper. If you would like to donate an item not listed, please add it to the list. Thank you for your support at this expensive time of year.

Bottle red wine	
Bottle white wine	
4 cans of beer	
4 cans of lager	
4 cans of cider	
Bottle of Buck's Fizz	
2 bottles of cola	
2 bottles of lemonade	
Christmas crackers	
Christmas napkins	
Christmas pudding	
Mince pies	
Christmas cake	
Box of chocolates	
Box of tea-bags	
Jar of coffee	
Box of biscuits	
2 6-packs of crisps	
2 large bags of peanuts	
2 tins of soup	
2 tins of fruit	
Tin of salmon	
2 jars of chutney	
After-dinner mints	
Calendar	

Children's Christmas hamper

Please sign against an item(s) that you are willing to contribute to our Children's Christmas hamper. If you would like to donate an item not listed, please add it to the list. Thank you for your support at this expensive time of year.

Christmas story-book	
Christmas story tape	
Seasonal balloons	
Selection box	
Child's calendar	
Mini Christmas cake	
Chocolate coins	
Large tube of sweets	
6-pack of juice	
Novelty pasta	
Christmas biscuits	
6-pack of crisps	
Pack of crayons	
Pack of felt-tipped pens	
Colouring book	
Jigsaw puzzle	
Pack of stickers	
Game of 'Snap'	
Magnetic letters	
Magnetic numbers	
Novelty socks	
Santa sack	
Santa hat	
Sleigh bells	

My favourites

SIDE A	SIDE B
_____	_____
_____	_____
_____	_____
_____	_____
_____	_____

's favourites

Teddy bear emotions game

Ladybird drive

Name............................

Head...6
Body...5
Spots...4
Legs...3
Eyes...2
Feelers...1

1	2	3
4	5	6

Cups and saucers

Children's quiz

1	Who sat on a tuffet?	
2	What is the name of the dog in the Tweenies?	
3	How many dwarfs did Snow White meet?	
4	Which of the Teletubbies has a scooter?	
5	Which Mr Man has very long arms?	
6	What could Dumbo do that other elephants can't?	
7	Who has Lofty, Dizzy and Scoop in his crew?	
8	What did Jack and Jill go up the hill for?	
9	What is Postman Pat's cat called?	
10	What number is Thomas The Tank Engine?	
11	How many little pigs did the wolf try to eat?	
12	What colour was Riding Hood's cloak?	
13	What was Humpty Dumpty?	
14	Who took two of each animal into the ark?	
15	Whose nose grew bigger when he told a lie?	

Family favourites quiz

Name: Contact Tel No:

1	Who first provided the voice for Thomas The Tank Engine?	
2	Name the two females in Scooby Doo.	
3	Robert, a true craftsman?	
4	On what day and time was Crackerjack?	
5	In the Lion King, who is Simba's evil uncle?	
6	Mr Hague & Mr Franklyn (to their friends)!	
7	What was the name of He-Man's castle?	
8	In the old TV test card, what game was the girl playing?	
9	Where would you find Sage, Dill and Basil here?	
10	What is Noo Noo in the Teletubbies?	
11	Mud and Bo – a childhood favourite!	
12	What's the name of Crystal Tip's dog?	
13	Which Mr Man is shown lying down on the back of the book?	
14	Who provided most of the voices for Will O' the Wisp?	
15	Which actor brought Aladdin's genie to life?	
16	Name the snail in The Magic Roundabout.	
17	An admirer, a hot beverage and a continent!	
18	Name the Seven Dwarfs.	
19	Which children's drama spawned Ant and Dec?	
20	Who were the four main characters in Rainbow?	
21	A bakery product donkey!	
22	Name the first cartoon in which Mickey Mouse starred.	
23	What's the name of the dog in the Tweenies?	
24	Name Harry Potter's loathsome cousin.	
25	What was Hartley in Pipkins?	
26	What's the top speed for Thunderbird 1?	
27	Which school did Tucker, Roly and Zammo attend?	
28	Sounds like a floating digit!	
29	If Mowgli's a man-cub and Baloo's a bear, what's King Louie?	
30	In the Roald Dahl novel, what does BFG stand for?	

Treasure map

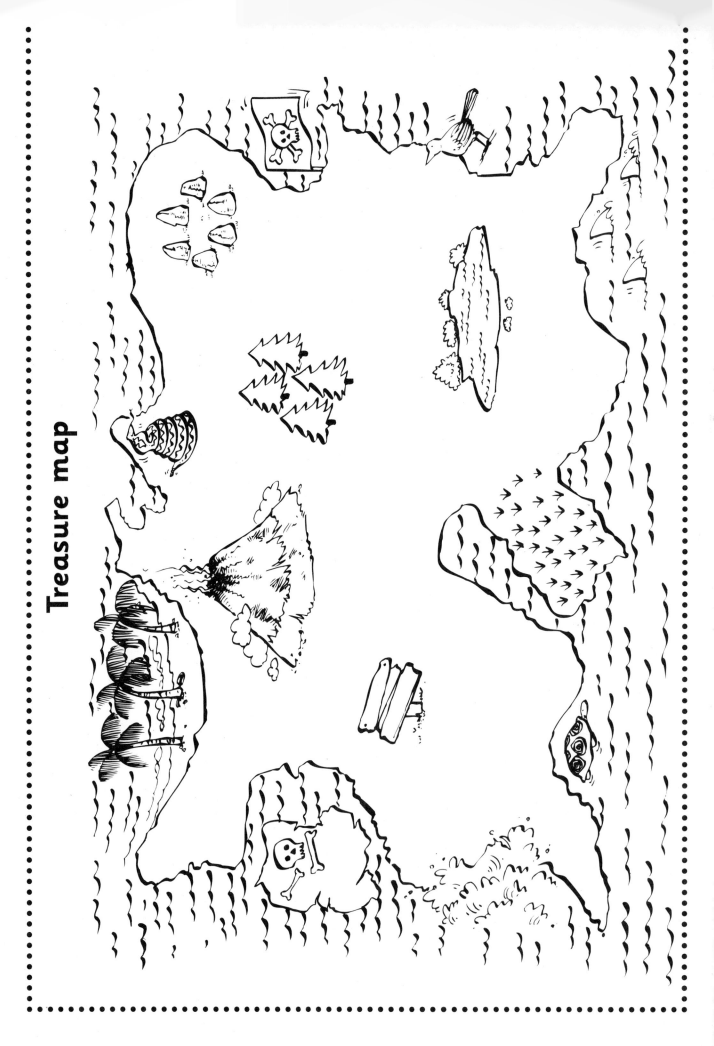